The Condition, Elevation, Emigration and Destiny of the Colored People of the United States

Martin R. Delany

Black Classic Press

The Condition, Elevation, Emigration and Destiny of the Colored People of the United States

Copyright 1993

All rights reserved

First published in 1852

Published in 1993 by Black Classic Press

Cover design by Ife Nii Owoo

Founded in 1978, Blacl ISBN 10: 0-933121-42-3   oring-
ing to light obscure arISBN: 13: 978-0-933121-42-3about
people of African descent. If our books are not available
in your area, ask your local bookseller to order them.
Our current list of titles can be obtained by writing:

Black Classic Press
c/o List
P.O. Box 13414
Baltimore, MD 21203-3414

A Young Press With Some Very Old Ideas

SINCERELY DEDICATED
TO THE AMERICAN PEOPLE,
NORTH AND SOUTH.

BY THEIR MOST DEVOUT,
AND PATRIOTIC FELLOW-CITIZEN,
THE AUTHOR.

CONTENTS.

PAGE

PREFACE, ... 7

CHAPTER I.
CONDITION OF MANY CLASSES IN EUROPE, ... 11

CHAPTER II.
COMPARATIVE CONDITION OF THE COLORED PEOPLE OF THE
UNITED STATES, ... 14

CHAPTER III.
AMERICAN COLONIZATION, ... 30

CHAPTER IV.
OUR ELEVATION IN THE UNITED STATES, ... 36

CHAPTER V.
MEANS OF ELEVATION, ... 41

CAHPTER VI.
THE UNITED STATES OUR COUNTRY, ... 48

CHAPTER VII.
CLAIMS OF COLORED MEN AS CITIZENS, ... 49

CHAPTER VIII.
COLORED AMERICAN WARRIORS, ... 67

CHAPTER IX.
CAPACITY OF COLORED MEN AND WOMEN AS CITIZEN MEM-
BERS OF COMMUNITY, ... 85

CHAPTER X.
PRACTICAL UTILITY OF COLORED PEOPLE OF THE PRESENT
DAY AS MEMBERS OF SOCIETY—BUSINESS MEN AND ME-
CHANICS, ... 92

CONTENTS.

CHAPTER XI.

LITERARY AND PROFESSIONAL COLORED MEN AND WOMEN,.. 110

CHAPTER XII.

STUDENTS OF VARIOUS PROFESSIONS, ... 134

CHAPTER XIII.

A SCAN AT PAST THINGS, ... 137

CHAPTER XIV.

LATE MEN OF LITERARY, PROFESSIONAL AND ARTISTIC NOTE, 141

CHAPTER XV.

FARMERS AND HERDSMEN, ... 144

CHAPTER XVI.

NATIONAL DISFRANCHISEMENT OF COLORED PEOPLE, ... 147

CHAPTER XVII.

EMIGRATION OF THE COLORED PEOPLE OF THE UNITED STATES, 159

CHAPTER XVIII.

" REPUBLIC OF LIBERIA," 160

CHAPTER XIX.

THE CANADAS, ... 173

CHAPTER XX.

CENTRAL AND SOUTH AMERICA AND THE WEST INDIES, ... 178

CHAPTER XXI.

NICARAGUA AND NEW GRENADA, ... 188

CHAPTER XXII.

THINGS AS THEY ARE,................................. 190

CHAPTER XXIII.

A GLANCE AT OURSELVES—CONCLUSION, ... 197

APPENDIX.

A PROJECT FOR AN EXPEDITION OF ADVENTURE TO THE
EASTERN COAST OF AFRICA, ... 209

PREFACE.

THE author of this little volume has no other apology for offering it to the public, than the hurried manner in which it has been composed. Being detained in the city of New York on business, he seized the opportunity of a tedious delay, and wrote the work in the inside of one month, attending to other business through the day, and lecturing on physiology sometimes in the evening. The reader will therefore not entertain an idea of elegance of language and terseness of style, such as should rule the sentences of every composition, by whomsoever written.

His sole object has been, to place before the public in general, and the colored people of the United States in particular, great truths concerning this class of citizens, which appears to have been heretofore avoided, as well by friends as enemies to their elevation. By opponents, to conceal information, that they are well aware would stimulate and impel them on to bold and adventurous deeds of manly daring; and by friends, who seem to have acted on the principle of the zealous orthodox, who would prefer losing the object of his pursuit to changing his policy.

There are also a great many colored people in the United States, who have independence of spirit, who desire to, and do, think for themselves; but for the want of general information, and in consequence of a prevailing opinion that has obtained, that no thoughts nor opinions must be expressed, even though it would eventuate in their elevation, except it emanate from some old, orthodox, stereotyped doctrine concerning them; therefore, such a work as this, which is but a mere introduction to what will henceforth emanate from the pen of colored men and women, appeared to be in most anxious demand, in order to settle their minds entirely, and concentrate them upon an effective and specific course of procedure. We have never conformed with that class of philosophers who would keep the people in ignorance, lest they might change their opinion from former predilections. This we shall never do, except pressing necessity demands it, and then only as a measure to prevent bad consequences, for the time.

The colored people of to-day are not the colored people of a quarter of a century ago, and require very different means and measures to satisfy their wants and demands, and to effect their advancement. No wise statesman presumes the same measures for the satisfaction of the American people now, that may have been with propriety adopted twenty-five years ago; neither is it wisdom to presume, that the privileges which satisfied colored people twenty years ago, they will be reconciled with now. That with which the father of the writer may have been satisfied, even up to the present day, the writer cannot be content with; the one lived in times antecedent to the birth of the other; that which answered then, does not answer now: so is it with the whole class of colored people in the United States. Their feelings, tastes, predilections, wants, demands, and sympathies, are identical, and homogeneous with those of all other Americans.

> "Fleecy locks and black complexion,
> Cannot alter nature's claim;
> Skins may differ, but affections,
> Dwell in black and white the same."

Many of the distinguished characters referred to in this work, who lived in former days, for which there is no credit given, have been obtained from various sources—as fragments of history, pamphlets, files of newspapers, obsolete American history, and some from Mrs. Child's Collection. Those of modern date, are living facts known to the writer in his travels through the United States, having been from Canada and Maine to Arkansas and Texas. The origin of the breast-works of cotton bales on Chalmet Plains, at the battle of New Orleans, the writer learned in that city, from old colored men in 1840, and subsequently, from other sources; as well as much useful information concerning that battle, from *Julien Bennoit,* spoken of in the work. He has before referred to it some five or six years ago, through the columns of a paper, of which he was then editor, and not until subsequently to his narrating the same facts in these columns, was he aware that it was ever mentioned in print, when he saw, on the 3d day of March, on looking over the contributions of the "Liberty Bell," a beautiful annual of Boston, the circumstance referred to by DAVID LEE CHILD, Esq., the particulars of which will be found in our version.

The original intention was to make this a pamphlet of a few pages, the writer commencing with that view; but finding that he could not thus justify the design of the work, will fully explain the cause of its present volume. The subject of this work is one that the writer has given thought for years, and the only regret that he has now in placing it before the public is, that his circumstances and engagements have not afforded him such time and opportunity as to do justice to it. But, should he succeed in turning the attention of the colored people, in general, in this direction—he shall have been amply compensated for the labor bestowed. An appendix will be found giving the plan of the author, laid out at twenty-four years of age, but subsequently improved on, for the elevation of the colored race. That plan of course, as this work will fully show, has been abandoned for a far more glorious one; albeit, we as a race, still lay claim to the project, which one day must be added to our dashing strides in national advancement, successful adventure, and unsurpassed enterprise.

One part of the American people, though living in near proximity and together, are quite unacquainted with the other; and one of the great objects of the author is, to make each acquainted. Except the character of an individual is known, there can be no just appreciation of his worth; and as with individuals, so is it with classes.

The colored people are not yet known, even to their most professed friends among the white Americans; for the reason, that politicians, religionists, colonizationists, and abolitionists, have each and all, at different times, presumed to *think* for, dictate to, and *know* better what suited colored people, than they knew for themselves; and consequently, there has been no other knowledge of them obtained, than that which has been obtained through these mediums. Their history—past, present, and future, has been written by them, who, for reasons well known, which are named in this volume, are not their representatives, aud, therefore, do not properly nor fairly present their wants and claims among their fellows. Of these impressions, we design disabusing the public mind, and correcting the false impressions of all classes upon this great subject. A moral and mental, is as obnoxious as a physical servitude, and not to be tolerated; as the one may, eventually, lead to the other. Of these we feel the direful effects.

> " If I'm designed your lordling's slave,
> By nature's law designed ;
> Why was an independent wish
> E'er planted in my mind ?"

CHAPTER I.

CONDITION OF MANY CLASSES IN EUROPE CONSIDERED.

THAT there have been in all ages and in all countries, in every quarter of the habitable globe, especially among those nations laying the greatest claim to civilization and enlightenment, classes of people who have been deprived of equal privileges, political, religious and social, cannot be denied, and that this deprivation on the part of the ruling classes is cruel and unjust, is also equally true. Such classes have ever been looked upon as inferior to their oppressors, and have ever been mainly the domestics and menials of society, doing the low offices and drudgery of those among whom they lived, moving about and existing by mere sufferance, having no rights nor privileges but those conceded by the common consent of their political superiors. These are historical facts that cannot be controverted, and therefore proclaim in tones more eloquently than thunder, the listful attention of every oppressed man, woman, and child under the government of the people of the United States of America.

In past ages there were many such classes, as the Israelites in Egypt, the Gladiators in Rome, and similar classes in Greece; and in the present age, the Gipsies in Italy and Greece, the Cossacs in Russia and Turkey, the Sclaves and Croats in the Germanic States, and the Welsh and Irish among the British, to say nothing of various other classes among other nations.

That there have in all ages, in almost every nation, existed a nation within a nation—a people who although forming a part and parcel of the population, yet were from force of circumstances, known by the peculiar position they occupied, forming in fact, by the deprivation of political equality with others, no part, and if any, but a restricted part of the body politic of such nations, is also true.

Such then are the Poles in Russia, the Hungarians in Austria, the Scotch, Irish, and Welsh in the United Kingdom, and such also are the Jews, scattered throughout not only the length and breadth of Europe, but almost the habitable globe, maintaining their national characteristics, and looking forward in high hopes of seeing the day when they may return to their former national position of self-government and independence, let that be in whatever part of the habitable world it may. This is the lot of these various classes of people in Europe, and it is not our intention here, to discuss the justice or injustice of the causes that have contributed to their degradation, but simply to set forth the undeniable facts, which are as glaring as the rays of a noon-day's sun, thereby to impress them indelibly on the mind of every reader of this pamphlet.

It is not enough, that these people are deprived of equal privileges by their rulers, but, the more effectually to succeed, the equality of these classes must be denied, and their inferiority by nature as distinct races, actually asserted. This policy is necessary to appease the opposition that might be interposed in their behalf. Wherever there is arbitrary rule, there must of necessity, on the part of the dominant classes, superiority be assumed. To assume superiority, is to deny the equality of others, and to deny their equality, is to premise their incapacity for self-government. Let this once be conceded, and there will be little or no sympathy for the oppressed, the oppressor being left to prescribe whatever terms at discretion for their government, suits his own purpose.

Such then is the condition of various classes in Europe ; yes, nations, for centuries within nations, even without the hope of redemption among those who oppress them. And however unfavorable their condition, there is none more so than that of the colored people of the United States.

CHAPTER II.

COMPARATIVE CONDITION OF THE COLORED PEOPLE OF
THE UNITED STATES.

THE United States, untrue to her trust and unfaithful to her professed principles of republican equality,
has also pursued a policy of political degradation to a
large portion of her native born countrymen, and that
class is the Colored People. Denied an equality not
only of political, but of natural rights, in common
with the rest of our fellow citizens, there is no species
of degradation to which we are not subject.

Reduced to abject slavery is not enough, the very
thought of which should awaken every sensibility of
our common nature ; but those of their descendants
who are freemen even in the non-slaveholding States,
occupy the very same position politically, religiously,
civilly and socially, (with but few exceptions,) as the
bondman occupies in the slave States.

In those States, the bondman is disfranchised, and
for the most part so are we. He is denied all civil,
religious, and social privileges, except such as he gets
by mere sufferance, and so are we. They have no
part nor lot in the government of the country, neither
have we. They are ruled and governed without representation, existing as mere nonentities among the
citizens, and excrescences on the body politic—a mere
dreg in community, and so are we. Where then is

our political superiority to the enslaved ? none, neither are we superior in any other relation to society, except that we are defacto masters of ourselves and joint rulers of our own domestic household, while the bondman's self is claimed by another, and his relation to his family denied him. What the unfortunate classes are in Europe, such are we in the United States, which is folly to deny, insanity not to understand, blindness not to see, and surely now full time that our eyes were opened to these startling truths, which for ages have stared us full in the face.

It is time that we had become politicians, we mean, to understand the political economy and domestic policy of nations ; that we had become as well as moral theorists, also the practical demonstrators of equal rights and self-government. Except we do, it is idle to talk about rights, it is mere chattering for the sake of being seen and heard—like the slave, saying something because his so called "master" said it, and saying just what he told him to say. Have we not now sufficient intelligence among us to understand our true position, to realise our actual condition, and determine for ourselves what is best to be done ? If we have not now, we never shall have, and should at once cease prating about our equality, capacity, and all that.

Twenty years ago, when the writer was a youth, his young and yet uncultivated mind was aroused, and his tender heart made to leap with anxiety in anticipation of the promises then held out by the prime movers in the cause of our elevation.

In 1830 the most intelligent and leading spirits

among the colored men in the United States, such as
James Forten, Robert Douglass, I. Bowers, A. D.
Shadd, John Peck, Joseph Cassey, and John B. Vashon of Pennsylvania; John T. Hilton, Nathaniel and
Thomas Paul, and James G. Barbodoes of Massachusetts; Henry Sipkins, Thomas Hamilton, Thomas L.
Jennings, Thomas Downing, Samuel E. Cornish, and
others of New York; R. Cooley and others of Maryland, and representatives from other States which cannot now be recollected, the data not being at hand,
assembled in the city of Philadelphia, in the capacity
of a National Convention, to " devise ways and means
for the bettering of our condition." These Conventions
determined to assemble annually, much talent, ability,
and energy of character being displayed ; when in 1831
at a sitting of the Convention in September, from their
previous pamphlet reports, much interest having been
created throughout the country, they were favored by
the presence of a number of whites, some of whom were
able and distinguished men, such as Rev. R. R. Gurley, Arthur Tappan, Elliot Cresson, John Rankin,
Simeon Jocelyn and others, among them William
Lloyd Garrison, then quite a young man, all of whom
were staunch and ardent Colonizationists, young Garrison at that time, doing his mightiest in his favorite
work.

Among other great projects of interest brought before
the convention at a previous sitting, was that of the expe-
diency of a general emigration, as far as it was practicable, of the colored people to the British Provinces of
North America. Another was that of raising sufficient

means for the establishment and erection of a College for the proper education of the colored youth. These gentlemen long accustomed to observation and reflection on the condition of their people, saw at once, that there must necessarily be means used adequate to the end to be attained—that end being an unqualified equality with the ruling class of their fellow citizens. He saw that as a class, the colored people of the country were ignorant, degraded and oppressed, by far the greater portion of them being abject slaves in the South, the very condition of whom was almost enough, under the circumstances, to blast the remotest hope of success, and those who were freemen, whether in the South or North, occupied a subservient, servile, and menial position, considering it a favor to get into the service of the whites, and do their degrading offices. That the difference between the whites and themselves, consisted in the superior advantages of the one over the other, in point of attainments. That if a knowledge of the arts and sciences, the mechanical occupations, the industrial occupations, as farming, commerce, and all the various business enterprises, and learned professions were necessary for the superior position occupied by their rulers, it was also necessary for them. And very reasonably too, the first suggestion which occurred to them was, the advantages of a location, then the necessity of a qualification. They reasoned with themselves, that all distinctive differences made among men on account of their origin, is wicked, unrighteous, and cruel, and never shall receive countenance in any shape from us, therefore, the first

acts of the measures entered into by them, was to protest, solemnly protest, against every unjust measure
and policy in the country, having for its object the
proscription of the colored people, whether state, national, municipal, social, civil, or religious.

But being far-sighted, reflecting, discerning men,
they took a political view of the subject, and determined for the good of their people to be governed in
their policy according to the facts as they presented
themselves.   In taking a glance at Europe, they
discovered there, however unjustly, as we have shown
in another part of this pamphlet, that there are and
have been numerous classes proscribed and oppressed,
and it was not for them to cut short their wise delibe-
rations, and arrest their proceedings in contention, as
to the cause, whether on account of language, the
color of eyes, hair, skin, or their origin of country—
because all this is contrary to reason, a contradiction
to common sense, at war with nature herself, and at
variance with facts as they stare us every day in the
face, among all nations, in every country—this being
made the pretext as a matter of *policy* alone—a fact
worthy of observation, that wherever the objects of
oppression are the most easily distinguished by any
peculiar or general characteristics, these people are
the more easily oppressed, because the war of oppression is the more easily waged against them.   This is
the case with the modern Jews and many other people
who have strongly-marked, peculiar, or distinguishing
characteristics.   This arises in this wise.   The policy
of all those who proscribe any people, induces them

to select as the objects of proscription, those who differed as much as possible, in some particulars, from themselves. This is to ensure the greater success, because it engenders the greater prejudice, or in other words, elicits less interest on the part of the oppressing class, in their favor. This fact is well understood in national conflicts, as the soldier or civilian, who is distinguished by his dress, mustache, or any other peculiar appendage, would certainly prove himself a madman, if he did not take the precaution to change his dress, remove his mustache, and conceal as much as possible his peculiar characteristics, to give him access among the repelling party. This is mere policy, nature having nothing to do with it. Still, it is a fact, a great truth well worthy of remark, and as such we adduce it for the benefit of those of our readers, unaccustomed to an enquiry into the policy of nations.

In view of these truths, our fathers and leaders in our elevation, discovered that as a policy, we the colored people were selected as the subordinate class in this country, not on account of any actual or supposed inferiority on their part, but simply because, in view of all the circumstances of the case, they were the very best class that could be selected. They would have as readily had any other class as subordinates in the country, as the colored people, but the condition of society *at the time*, would not admit of it. In the struggle for American Independence, there were among those who performed the most distinguished parts, the most common-place peasantry of the Provinces. English, Danish, Irish, Scotch, and others, were among those whose names blazoned forth as heroes in the American Revolution. But a single reflection will convince us, that no course of policy could have induced the proscription of the parentage and relatives of such men as Benjamin Franklin the printer, Roger Sherman the cobbler, the tinkers, and others of the signers of the Declaration of Independence. But as they were determined to have a subservient class, it will readily be conceived, that according to the state of society at the time, the better policy on their part was, to select some class, who from their political position—however much they may have contributed their aid as we certainly did, in the general struggle for liberty by force of arms—who had the least claims upon them, or who had the *least chance*, or was the *least potent* in urging their claims. This class of course was the colored people and Indians.

The Indians who in the early settlement of the continent, before an African captive had ever been introduced thereon, were reduced to the most abject slavery, toiling day and night in the mines, under the relentless hands of heartless Spanish taskmasters, but being a race of people raised to the sports of fishing, the chase, and of war, were wholly unaccustomed to labor, and therefore sunk under the insupportable weight, two millions and a half having fallen victims to the cruelty of oppression and toil suddenly placed upon their shoulders. And it was only this that prevented their farther enslavement as a class, after the provinces were absolved from the British Crown.   It is true that their general enslavement took place on the islands and in the mining districts of South America, where indeed, the Europeans continued to enslave them, until a comparatively recent period; still, the design, the feeling, and inclination from policy, was the same to do so here, in this section of the continent.

Nor was it until their influence became too great, by the political position occupied by their brethren in the new republic, that the German and Irish peasantry ceased to be sold as slaves for a term of years fixed by law, for the repayment of their passage-money, the descendants of these classes of people for a long time being held as inferiors, in the estimation of the ruling class, and it was not until they assumed the rights and privileges guaranteed to them by the established policy of the country, among the leading spirits of whom were their relatives, that the policy towards them was discovered to be a bad one, and accordingly changed.   Nor was it, as is frequently very erroneously asserted, by colored as well as white persons, that it was on account of hatred to the African, or in other words, on account of hatred to his color, that the African was selected as the subject of oppression in this country.   This is sheer nonsense; being based on policy and nothing else, as shown in another place. The Indians, who being the most foreign to the sympathies of the Europeans on this continent, were selected in the first place, who, being unable to withstand the hardships, gave way before them.

But the African race had long been known to
Europeans, in all ages of the world's history, as a
long-lived, hardy race, subject to toil and labor of
various kinds, subsisting mainly by traffic, trade, and
industry, and consequently being as foreign to the
sympathies of the invaders of the continent as the
Indians, they were selected, captured, brought here
as a laboring class, and as a matter of policy held
as such. Nor was the absurd idea of natural
inferiority of the African ever dreamed of, until
recently adduced by the slave-holders and their
abettors, in justification of their policy. This, with
contemptuous indignation, we fling back into their
face, as a scorpion to a vulture. And so did our
patriots and leaders in the cause of regeneration
know better, and never for a moment yielded to the
base doctrine. But they had discovered the great
fact, that a cruel policy was pursued towards our
people, and that they possessed distinctive characteristics which made them the objects of proscription.
These characteristics being strongly marked in the
colored people, as in the Indians, by color, character
of hair and so on, made them the more easily distinguished from other Americans, and the policies
more effectually urged against us. For this reason
they introduced the subject of emigration to Canada,
and a proper institution for the education of the youth.

At this important juncture of their proceedings,
the afore named white gentlemen were introduced to
the notice of the Convention, and after gaining permission to speak, expressed their gratification and

surprise at the qualification and talent manifested by different members of the Convention, all expressing their determination to give the cause of the colored people more serious reflection. Mr. Garrison, the youngest of them all, and none the less honest on account of his youthfulness, being but 26 years of age at the time, (1831) expressed his determination to change his course of policy at once, and espouse the cause of the elevation of the colored people here in their own country. We are not at present well advised upon this point, it now having escaped our memory, but we are under the impression that Mr. Jocelyn also, at once changed his policy.

During the winter of 1832, Mr. Garrison issued his " Thoughts on African Colonization," and near about the same time or shortly after, issued the first number of the "Liberator," in both of which, his full convic- tions of the enormity of American slavery, and the wickedness of their policy towards the colored people, were fully expressed. At the sitting of the Conven- tion in this year, a number, perhaps all of these gentlemen were present, and those who had denounced the Colonization scheme, and espoused the cause of the elevation of the colored people in this country, or the Anti Slavery cause, as it was now termed, expressed themselves openly and without reserve.

Sensible of the high-handed injustice done to the colored people in the United States, and the mischief likely to emanate from the unchristian proceedings of the deceptious Colonization scheme, like all honest hearted penitents, with the ardor only known to new converts, they entreated the Convention, whatever they did, not to entertain for a moment, the idea of recommending emigration to their people, nor the establishment of separate institutions of learning. They earnestly contended, and doubtless honestly meaning what they said, that they (the whites) had been our oppressors and injurers, they had obstructed our progress to the high positions of civilization, and now, it was their bounden duty to make full amends for the injuries thus inflicted on an unoffending people. They exhorted the Convention to cease ; as they had laid on the burden, they would also take it off; as they had obstructed our pathway, they would remove the hindrance. In a word, as they had oppressed and trampled down the colored people, they would now elevate them. These suggestions and promises, good enough to be sure, after they were made, were accepted by the Convention—though some gentlemen were still in favor of the first project as the best policy, Mr. A. D. Shadd of West Chester, Pa., as we learn from himself, being one among that number— ran through the country like wild-fire, no one thinking, and if he thought, daring to speak above his breath of going any where out of certain prescribed limits, or of sending a child to school, if it should but have the name of "colored" attached to it, without the risk of being termed a "traitor" to the cause of his people, or an enemy to the Anti Slavery cause.

At this important point in the history of our efforts, the colored men stopped suddenly, and with their hands thrust deep in their breeches-pockets, and their mouths gaping open, stood gazing with astonishment, wonder, and surprise, at the stupendous moral colossal statues of our Anti-Slavery friends and brethren, who in the heat and zeal of honest hearts, from a desire to make atonement for the many wrongs inflicted, promised a great deal more than they have ever been able half to fulfill, in thrice the period in which they expected it. And in this, we have no fault to find with our Anti-Slavery friends, and here wish it to be understood, that we are not laying any thing to their charge as blame, neither do we desire for a moment to reflect on them, because we heartily believe that all that they did at the time, they did with the purest and best of motives, and further believe that they now are, as they then were, the truest friends we have among the whites in this country. And hope, and desire, and request, that our people should always look upon *true* anti-slavery people, Abolitionists we mean, as their friends, until they have just cause for acting otherwise. It is true, that the Anti-Slavery, like all good causes, has produced some recreants, but the cause itself is no more to be blamed for that, than Christianity is for the malconduct of any professing hypocrite, nor the society of Friends, for the conduct of a broad-brimmed hat and shad-belly coated horse-thief, because he spoke *thee* and *thou* before stealing the horse. But what is our condition even amidst our Anti-Slavery friends ? And here, as our sole intention is to contribute to the elevation of our people, we must be permitted to express our opinion freely, without being thought uncharitable.

In the first place, we should look at the objects for which the Anti-Slavery cause was commenced, and the promises or inducements it held out at the commencement. It should be borne in mind, that Anti-Slavery took its rise among *colored men*, just at the time they were introducing their greatest projects for their own elevation, and that our Anti-Slavery brethren were converts of the colored men, in behalf of their elevation. Of course, it would be expected that being baptized into the new doctrines, their faith would induce them to embrace the principles therein contained, with the strictest possible adherence.

The cause of dissatisfaction with our former condition, was, that we were proscribed, debarred, and shut out from every respectable position, occupying the places of inferiors and menials.

It was expected that Anti-Slavery, according to its professions, would extend to colored persons, as far as in the power of its adherents, those advantages nowhere else to be obtained among white men. That colored boys would get situations in their shops and stores, and every other advantage tending to elevate them as far as possible, would be extended to them. At least, it was expected, that in Anti-Slavery establishments, colored men would have the preference. Because, there was no other ostensible object in view, in the commencement of the Anti-Slavery enterprise, than the *elevation* of the *colored man*, by facilitating his efforts in attaining to equality with the white man. It was urged, and it was true, that the colored people were susceptible of all that the whites were, and all that was required was to give them a fair opportunity, and they would prove their capacity. That it was unjust, wicked, and cruel, the result of an unnatural prejudice, that debarred them from places of respectability, and that public opinion could and should be corrected upon this subject. That it was only necessary to make a sacrifice of feeling, and an innovation on the customs of society, to establish a different order of things,—that as Anti-Slavery men, they were willing to make these sacrifices, and determined to take the colored man by the hand, making common cause with him in affliction, and bear a part of the odium heaped upon him. That his cause was the cause of God—that " In as much as ye did it not unto the least of these my little ones, ye did it not unto me," and that as Anti-Slavery men, they would " do right if the heavens fell." Thus, was the cause espoused, and thus did we expect much. But in all this, we were doomed to disappointment, sad, sad disappointment. Instead of realising what we had hoped for, we find ourselves occupying the very same position in relation to our Anti-Slavery friends, as we do in relation to the pro-slavery part of the community—a mere secondary, underling position, in all our relations to them, and any thing more than this, is not a matter of course affair—it comes not by established anti-slavery custom or right, but like that which emanates from the proslavery portion of the community, by mere sufferance.

It is true, that the " Liberator" office, in Boston, has got Elijah Smith, a colored youth, at the cases

—the "Standard," in New York, a young colored man, and the "Freeman," in Philadelphia, William Still, another, in the publication office, as "packing clerk;" yet these are but three out of the hosts that fill these offices in their various departments, all occupying places that could have been, and as we once thought, would have been, easily enough, occupied by colored men. Indeed, we can have no other idea about anti-slavery in this country, than that the legitimate persons to fill any and every position about an anti-slavery establishment are colored persons. Nor will it do to argue in extenuation, that white men are as justly entitled to them as colored men; because white men do not from *necessity* become anti-slavery men in order to get situations; they being white men, may occupy any position they are capable of filling—in a word, their chances are endless, every avenue in the country being opened to them. They do not therefore become abolitionists, for the sake of employment—at least, it is not the song that anti-slavery sung, in the first love of the new faith, proclaimed by its disciples.

And if it be urged that colored men are incapable as yet to fill these positions, all that we have to say is, that the cause has fallen far short; almost equivalent to a failure, of a tithe, of what it promised to do in half the period of its existence, to this time, if it have not as yet, now a period of twenty years, raised up colored men enough, to fill the offices within its patronage. We think it is not unkind to say, if it had been half as faithful to itself, as it

should have been—its professed principles we mean ;
it could have reared and tutored from childhood,
colored men enough by this time, for its own especial
purpose. These we know could have been easily
obtained, because colored people in general, are
favorable to the anti-slavery cause, and wherever
there is an adverse manifestation, it arises from sheer
ignorance ; and we have now but comparatively few
such among us. There is one thing certain, that no
colored person, except such as would reject education
altogether, would be adverse to putting their child
with an anti-slavery person, for educational advantages. This then, could have been done. But it has
not been done, and let the cause of it be whatever
it may, and let whoever may be to blame, we are
willing to let all that pass, and extend to our anti-
slavery brethren the right-hand of fellowship, bidding
them God-speed in the propagation of good and
wholesome sentiments—for whether they are practically carried out or not, the professions are in themselves all right and good. Like Christianity, the
principles are holy and of divine origin. And we
believe, if ever a man started right, with pure and
holy motives, Mr. Garrison did ; and that, had he
the power of making the cause what it should be, it
would all be right, and there never would have been
any cause for the remarks we have made, though in
kindness, and with the purest of motives. We are
nevertheless, still occupying a miserable position in
the community, wherever we live ; and what we most
desire is, to draw the attention of our people to this

fact, and point out what, in our opinion, we conceive
to be a proper remedy.

———◦•◦———

CHAPTER III.

AMERICAN COLONIZATION.

WHEN we speak of colonization, we wish distinctly
to be understood, as speaking of the " American Colonization Society"—or that which is under its influence
—commenced in Richmond, Virginia, in 1817, under
the influence of Mr. Henry Clay of Ky., Judge
Bushrod Washington of Va., and other Southern
slaveholders, having for their express object, as their
speeches and doings all justify us in asserting in good
faith, the removal of the free colored people from the
ʼnd of their birth, for the security of the slaves, as
ʼerty to the slave propagandists.

This scheme had no sooner been propagated, than
the old and leading colored men of Philadelphia, Pa.,
with Richard Allen, James Forten, and others at their
head, true to their trust and the cause of their brethren, summoned the colored people together, and then
and there, in language and with voices pointed and
loud, protested against the scheme as an outrage,
having no other object in view, than the benefit of the
slave-holding interests of the country, and that as

freemen, they would never prove recreant to the cause of their brethren in bondage, by leaving them without hope of redemption from their chains. This determination of the colored patriots of Philadelphia was published in full, authentically, and circulated throughout the length and breadth of the country by the papers of the day. The colored people every where received the news, and at once endorsed with heart and soul, the doings of the Anti-Colonization Meeting of colored freemen. From that time forth, the colored people generally have had no sympathy with the colonization scheme, nor confidence in its leaders, looking upon them all, as arrant hypocrites, seeking every opportunity to deceive them. In a word, the monster was crippled in its infancy, and has never as yet recovered from the stroke. It is true, that like its ancient sire, that was "more subtile than all the beasts of the field," it has inherited a large portion of his most prominent characteristic—an idiosyncrasy with the animal—that enables him to entwine himself into the greater part of the Church and other institutions of the country, which having once entered there, leaves his venom, which put such a spell on the conductors of those institutions, that it is only on condition that a colored person consents to go to the neighborhood of his kindred brother monster the boa, that he may find admission in the one or the other. We look upon the American Colonization Society as one of the most arrant enemies of the colored man, ever seeking to discomfit him, and envying him of every privilege that he may enjoy. We believe it to be anti-Christian in its charac

ter, and misanthropic in its pretended sympathies.
Because if this were not the case, men could not be
found professing morality and Christianity—as to our
astonishment we have found them—who unhesitatingly
say, " I know it is right"—that is in itself—" to do"
so and so, " and I am willing and ready to do it, but
only on condition, that you go to Africa." Indeed, a
highly talented clergyman, informed us in November
last (three months ago) in the city of Philadelphia,
that he was present when the Rev. Doctor J. P. Durbin, late President of Dickinson College, called on
Rev. Mr. P. of B., to consult him about going to Liberia, to take charge of the literary department of an
University in contemplation, when the following conversation ensued : Mr. P. —" Doctor, I have as much
and more than I can do here, in educating the youth
of our own country, and preparing them for usefulness
here at home." Dr. D.—"Yes, but do as you may,
you can never be elevated here." Mr. P.—" Doctor,
do you not believe that the religion of our blessed
Redeemer Jesus Christ, has morality, humanity,
philanthropy, and justice enough in it to elevate us,
and enable us to obtain our rights in this our own
country ?" Dr. D.—" No, indeed, sir, I do not, and
if you depend upon that, your hopes are vain !"
Mr. P.—Turning to Doctor Durbin, looking him
solemnly, though affectionately in the face, remarked
—" Well, Doctor Durbin, we both profess to be minis-
ters of Christ ; but dearly as I love the cause of my
Redeemer, if for a moment, I could entertain the
opinion you do about Christianity, I would not serve

him another hour!" We do not know, as we were
not advised, that the Rev. doctor added in fine,—
"Well, you may quit now, for all your serving him
will not avail against the power of the god (hydra)
of Colonization." Will any one doubt for a single
moment, the justice of our strictures on colonization,
after reading the conversation between the Rev. Dr.
Durbin and the colored clergyman? Surely not. We
can therefore make no account of it, but that of setting it down as being the worst enemy of the colored
people.

Recently, there has been a strained effort in the
city of New York on the part of the Rev. J. B. Pinney
and others, of the leading white colonizationists, to
get up a movement among some poor pitiable colored
men—we say pitiable, for certainly the colored persons who are at this period capable of loaning themselves to the enemies of their race, against the best
interest of all that we hold sacred to that race, are
pitiable in the lowest extreme, far beneath the dignity
of an enemy, and therefore, we pass them by with the
simple remark, that this is the hobby that colonization
is riding all over the country, as the "tremendous"
access of colored people to their cause within the last
twelve months. We should make another remark here
perhaps, in justification of governor Pinney's New
York allies—that is, report says, that in the short
space of some three or five months, one of his confi-
dants, benefited himself to the "reckoning" of from
eleven to fifteen hundred dollars, or "such a matter,
"while others were benefited in sums "pretty consid-

erable" but of a less "reckoning." Well, we do not
know after all, that they may not have quite as good
a right, to pocket part of the spoils of this "grab
game," as any body else. However, they are of little
consequence, as the ever watchful eye of those excellent gentlemen and faithful guardians of their people's
rights—the *Committee of Thirteen*, consisting of
Messrs. John J. Zuille, *Chairman*, T. Joiner White,
Philip A. Bell, *Secretaries*, Robert Hamilton, George
T. Downing, Jeremiah Powers, John T. Raymond,
Wm. Burnett, James McCuen Smith, Ezekiel Dias,
Junius C. Morel, Thomas Downing, and Wm. J. Wilson, have properly chastised this pet-slave of Mr.
Pinney, and made it "know its place," by keeping
within the bounds of its master's enclosure.

In expressing our honest conviction of the design-
edly injurious character of the Colonization Society,
we should do violence to our own sense of individual justice, if we did not express the belief, that
there are some honest hearted men, who not having
seen things in the proper light, favor that scheme, simply as a means of elevating the colored people. Such
persons, so soon as they become convinced of their
error, immediately change their policy, and advocate
the elevation of the colored people, anywhere and
everywhere, in common with other men. Of such
were the early abolitionists as before stated ; and the
great and good Dr. F. J. Lemoyne, Gerrit Smith,
and Rev. Charles Avery, and a host of others, who
were Colonizationists, before espousing the cause of
our elevation, here at home, and nothing but an honor-

able sense of justice, induces us to make these exceptions, as there are many good persons within our knowledge, whom we believe to be well wishers of the colored people, who may favor colonization.* But the animal itself is the same " hydra-headed monster," let whomsoever may fancy to pet it. A serpent is a serpent, and none the less a viper, because nestled in the bosom of an honest hearted man. This the colored people must bear in mind, and keep clear of the hideous thing, lest its venom may be tost upon them. But why deem any argument necessary to show the unrighteousness of colonization? Its very origin as before shown—the source from whence it sprung, being the offspring of slavery—is in itself, sufficient to blast it in the estimation of every colored person in the United States, who has sufficient intelligence to comprehend it.

* Benjamin Coates, Esq., a merchant of Philadelphia, we believe to be an honest hearted man, and real friend of the colored people, and a true, though as yet, rather undecided philanthropist. Mr. Coates, to our knowledge, has supported three or four papers published by colored men, for the elevation of colored people in the United States, and given, as he continues to do, considerable sums to their support. We have recently learned from himself, that, though he still advocates Colonization, simply as a means of elevating the colored race of the United States, that he has *left* the Colonization Society, and prefers seeing colored people located on this continent, to going to Liberia, or elsewhere off of it—though his zeal for the enlightenment of Africa, is unabated, as every good man's should be ; and we are satisfied, that Mr. Coates is neither well understood, nor rightly appreciated by the friends of our cause. One thing we do know, that he left the Colonization Society, because he could not conscientiously subscribe to its measures.

We dismiss this part of the subject, and proceed to consider the mode and means of our elevation in the United States.

———◦●◦———

CHAPTER IV.

OUR ELEVATION IN THE UNITED STATES.

THAT very little comparatively as yet has been done, to attain a respectable position as a class in this country, will not be denied, and that the successful accomplishment of this end is also possible, must also be admitted; but in what manner, and by what means, has long been, and is even now, by the best thinking minds among the colored people themselves, a matter of difference of opinion.

We believe in the universal equality of man, and believe in that declaration of God's word, in which it is there positively said, that " God has made of one blood all the nations that dwell on the face of the earth." Now of " the nations that dwell on the face of the earth," that is, all the people—there are one thousand millions of souls, and of this vast number of human beings, two-thirds are colored, from black, tending in complexion to the olive or that of the Chinese, with all the intermediate and admixtures of black and white, with the various " crosses" as they are physiologically, but erroneously termed, to white. We are thus explicit in stating these points, because we are determined to be understood by all. We have then, two colored to one white person throughout the earth, and yet, singular as it may appear, according to the present geographical and political history of the world, the white race predominates over the colored; or in other words, wherever there is one white person, that one rules and governs two colored persons. This is a living undeniable truth, to which we call the especial attention of the colored reader in particular. Now there is a cause for this, as there is no effect without a cause, a comprehensible remediable cause. We all believe in the justice of God, that he is impartial, "looking upon his children with an eye of care," dealing out to them all, the measure of his goodness ; yet, how can we reconcile ourselves to the difference that exists between the colored and the white races, as they truthfully present themselves before our eyes ? To solve this problem, is to know the remedy ; and to know it, is but necessary, in order successfully to apply it. And we shall but take the colored people of the United States, as a fair sample of the colored races everywhere of the present age, as the arguments that apply to the one, will apply to the other, whether Christians, Mahomedans, or pagans.

The colored races are highly susceptible of religion ; it is a constituent principle of their nature, and an excellent trait in their character. But unfortunately for them, they carry it too far. Their hope is largely de-

veloped, and consequently, they usually stand still—
hope in God, and really expect Him to do that for
them, which it is necessary they should do themselves.
This is their great mistake, and arises from a miscon-
ception of the character and ways of Deity. We must
know God, that is understand His nature and purposes, in order to serve Him ; and to serve Him well, is
but to know him rightly. To depend for assistance
upon God, is a *duty* and right; but to know when,
how, and in what manner to obtain it, is the key to
this great Bulwark of Strength, and Depository of
Aid.

God himself is perfect; perfect in all his works
and ways. He has means for every end ; and every
means used must be adequate to the end to be gained.
God's means are laws—fixed laws of nature, a part of
His own being, and as immutable, as unchangeable as
Himself. Nothing can be accomplished but through
the medium of, and conformable to these laws.

They are *three*—and like God himself, represented
in the three persons in the God-head—the *Spiritual*,
Moral and *Physical* Laws.

That which is Spiritual, can only be accomplished
through the medium of the Spiritual law; that which is
Moral, through the medium of the Moral law ; and that
which is Physical, through the medium of the Physical law. Otherwise than this, it is useless to expect
any thing. Does a person want a spiritual blessing,
he must apply through the medium of the spiritual
law—*pray* for it in order to obtain it. If they desire
to do a moral good, they must apply through the me-

dium of the moral law—exercise their sense and feeling of *right* and *justice*, in order to effect it. Do they want to attain a physical end, they can only do so through the medium of the physical law—go to *work* with muscles, hands, limbs, might and strength, and this, and nothing else will attain it.

The argument that man must pray for what he receives, is a mistake, and one that is doing the colored people especially, incalculable injury. That man must pray in order to get to Heaven, every Christian will admit—but a great truth we have yet got to learn, that he can live on earth whether he is religious or not, so that he conforms to the great law of God, regulating the things of earth ; the great physical laws. It is only necessary, in order to convince our people of their error and palpable mistake in this matter, to call their attention to the fact, that there are no people more religious in this Country, than the colored people, and none so poor and miserable as they. That prosperity and wealth, smiles upon the efforts of wicked white men, whom we know to utter the name of God with curses, instead of praises. That among the slaves, there are thousands of them religious, continually raising their voices, sending up their prayers to God, invoking His aid in their behalf, asking for a speedy deliverance ; but they are still in chains, although they have thrice suffered out their three score years and ten. That " God sendeth rain upon the just and unjust," should be sufficient to convince us that our success in life, does not depend upon our religious character, but that the physical laws governing all earthly and temporary affairs, benefit equally the just and the unjust. Any other doctrine than this, is downright delusion, unworthy of a free people, and only intended for slaves. That all men and women, should be moral, upright, good and religious—we mean *Christians*—we would not utter a word against, and could only wish that it were so; but, what we here desire to do is, to correct the long standing error among a large body of the colored people in this country, that the cause of our oppression and degradation, is the displeasure of God towards us, because of our unfaithfulness to Him. This is not true; because if God is just—and he is—there could be no justice in prospering white men with his fostering care, for more than two thousand years, in all their wickedness, while dealing out to the colored people, the measure of his displeasure, for not half the wickedness as that of the whites. Here then is our mistake, and let it forever henceforth be corrected. We are no longer slaves, believing any interpretation that our oppressors may give the word of God, for the purpose of deluding us to the more easy subjugation; but freemen, comprising some of the first minds of intelligence and rudimental qualifications, in the country. What then is the remedy, for our degradation and oppression? This appears now to be the only remaining question —the means of successful elevation in this our own native land? This depends entirely upon the application of the means of Elevation.

CHAPTER V.

MEANS OF ELEVATION.

MORAL theories have long been resorted to by us, as a means of effecting the redemption of our brethren in bonds, and the elevation of the free colored people in this country. Experience has taught us, that speculations are not enough; that the *practical* application of principles adduced, the thing carried out, is the only true and proper course to pursue.

We have speculated and moralised much about equality—claiming to be as good as our neighbors, and every body else—all of which, may do very well in ethics—but not in politics. We live in society among men, conducted by men, governed by rules and regulations. However arbitrary, there are certain policies that regulate all well organized institutions and corporate bodies. We do not intend here to speak of the legal political relations of society, for those are treated on elsewhere. The business and social, or voluntary and mutual policies, are those that now claim our attention. Society regulates itself—being governed by mind, which like water, finds its own level. " Like seeks like," is a principle in the laws of matter, as well as of mind. There is such a thing as inferiority of things, and positions; at least society has made them so ; and while we continue to live among men, we must agree to all *just* measures—

all those we mean, that do not necessarily infringe on the rights of others. By the regulations of society, there is no equality of persons, where there is not an equality of attainments. By this, we do not wish to be understood as advocating the actual equal attainments of every individual ; but we mean to say, that if these attainments be necessary for the elevation of the white man, they are necessary for the elevation of the colored man. That some colored men and women, in a like proportion to the whites, should be qualified in all the attainments possessed by them. It is one of the regulations of society the world over, and we shall have to conform to it, or be discarded as unworthy of the associations of our fellows.

Cast our eyes about us and reflect for a moment, and what do we behold ! every thing that presents to view gives evidence of the skill of the white man. Should we purchase a pound of groceries, a yard of linen, a vessel of crockeryware, a piece of furniture, the very provisions that we eat,—all, all are the products of the white man, purchased by us from the white man, consequently, our earnings and means, are all given to the white man.

Pass along the avenues of any city or town, in which you live—behold the trading shops—the manufactories—see the operations of the various machinery —see the stage-coaches coming in, bringing the mails of intelligence—look at the railroads interlining every section, bearing upon them their mighty trains, flying with the velocity of the swallow, ushering in the hundreds of industrious, enterprising travellers.

Cast again your eyes widespread over the ocean—see the vessels in every direction with their white sheets spread to the winds of heaven, freighted with the commerce, merchandise and wealth of many nations. Look as you pass along through the cities, at the great and massive buildings—the beautiful and extensive structures of architecture—behold the ten thousand cupolas, with their spires all reared up towards heaven, intersecting the territory of the clouds—all standing as mighty living monuments, of the industry, enterprise, and intelligence of the white man. And yet, with all these living truths, rebuking us with scorn, we strut about, place our hands akimbo, straighten up ourselves to our greatest height, and talk loudly about being " as good as any body." How do we compare with them ? Our fathers are their coachmen, our brothers their cookmen, and ourselves their waiting-men. Our mothers their nurse-women, our sisters their scrub-women, our daughters their maid-women, and our wives their washer-women. Until colored men, attain to a position above permitting their mothers, sisters, wives, and daughters, to do the drudgery and menial offices of other men's wives and daughters; it is useless, it is nonsense, it is pitiable mockery, to talk about equality and elevation in society. The world is looking upon us, with feelings of commisseration, sorrow, and contempt. We scarcely deserve sympathy, if we peremptorily refuse advice, bearing upon our elevation.

We will suppose a case for argument : In this city

reside, two colored families, of three sons and three daughters each. At the head of each family, there is an old father and mother. The opportunities of these families, may or may not be the same for educational advantages—be that as it may, the children of the one go to school, and become qualified for the duties of life. One daughter becomes school-teacher, another a mantua-maker, and a third a fancy shop-keeper; while one son becomes a farmer, another a merchant, and a third a mechanic. All enter into business with fine prospects, marry respectably, and settle down in domestic comfort—while the six sons and daughters of the other family, grow up without educational and business qualifications, and the highest aim they have, is to apply to the sons and daughters of the first named family, to hire for domestics! Would there be an equality here between the children of these two families? Certainly not. This, then, is precisely the position of the colored people generally in the United States, compared with the whites. What is necessary to be done,.in order to attain an equality, is to change the condition, and the person is at once changed. If, as before stated, a knowledge of all the various business enterprises, trades, professions, and sciences, is necessary for the elevation of the white, a knowledge of them also is necessary for the elevation of the colored man; and he cannot be elevated without them.

White men are producers—we are consumers. They build houses, and we rent them. They raise produce, and we consume it. They manufacture clothes and wares, and we garnish ourselves with them. They build coaches, vessels, cars, hotels, saloons, and other vehicles and places of accommodation, and we deliberately wait until they have got them in readiness, then walk in, and contend with as much assurance for a "right," as though the whole thing was bought by, paid for, and belonged to us. By their literary attainments, they are the contributors to, authors and teachers of, literature, science, religion, law, medicine, and all other useful attainments that the world now makes use of. We have no reference to ancient times—we speak of modern things.

These are the means by which God intended man to succeed: and this discloses the secret of the white man's success with all of his wickedness, over the head of the colored man, with all of his religion. We have been pointed and plain, on this part of the subject, because we desire our readers to see persons and things in their true position. Until we are determined to change the condition of things, and raise ourselves above the position in which we are now prostrated, we must hang our heads in sorrow, and hide our faces in shame. It is enough to know that these things are so ; the causes we care little about. Those we have been examining, complaining about, and moralising over, all our life time. This we are weary of. What we desire to learn now is, how to effect a *remedy ;* this we have endeavored to point out. Our elevation must be the result of *self-efforts*, and work of our *own hands*. No other human

power can accomplish it.   If we but determine it
shall be so, it will be so.   Let each one make the
case his own, and endeavor to rival his neighbor, in
honorable competition.

These are the proper and only means of elevating
ourselves and attaining equality in this country or
any other, and it is useless, utterly futile, to think
about going any where, except we are determined to
use these as the necessary means of developing our
manhood.   The means are at hand, within our reach.
Are we willing to try them ?   Are we willing to raise
ourselves superior to the condition of slaves, or continue the meanest underlings, subject to the beck
and call of every creature bearing a pale complexion ?
If we are, we had as well remained in the South, as
to have come to the North in search of more freedom.
What was the object of our parents in leaving the
south, if it were not for the purpose of attaining
equality in common with others of their fellow citizens,
by giving their children access to all the advantages
enjoyed by others ?   Surely this was their object.
They heard of liberty and equality here, and they
hastened on to enjoy it, and no people are more
astonished and disappointed than they, who for the
first time, on beholding the position we occupy here
in the free north—what is called, and what they
expect to find, the free States.   They at once tell us,
that they have as much liberty in the south as we
have in the north—that there as free people, they are
protected in their rights—that we have nothing more
—that in other respects they have the same opportu-

nity, indeed the preferred opportunity, of being their maids, servants, cooks, waiters, and menials in general, there, as we have here—that had they known for a moment, before leaving, that such was to be the only position they occupied here, they would have remained where they were, and never left. Indeed, such is the disappointment in many cases, that they immediately return back again, completely insulted at the idea, of having us here at the north, assume ourselves to be their superiors. Indeed, if our superior advantages of the free States, do not induce and stimulate us to the higher attainments in life, what in the name of degraded humanity will do it? Nothing, surely nothing. If, in fine, the advantages of free schools in Massachusetts, New York, Pennsylvania, Ohio, Michigan, and wherever else we may have them, do not give us advantages and pursuits superior to our slave brethren, then are the unjust assertions of Messrs. Henry Clay, John C. Calhoun, Theodore Frelinghuysen, late Governor Poindexter of Mississippi, George McDuffy, Governor Hammond of South Carolina, Extra Billy (present Governor) Smith, of Virginia, and the host of our oppressors, slave-holders and others, true, that we are insusceptible and incapable of elevation to the more respectable, honorable, and higher attainments among white men. But this we do not believe—neither do you, although our whole life and course of policy in this country are such, that it would seem to prove otherwise. The degradation of the slave parent has been entailed upon the child, induced by the subtle policy of the

oppressor, in regular succession handed down from
father to son—a system of regular submission and
servitude, menialism and dependence, until it has
become almost a physiological function of our system,
an actual condition of our nature. Let this no longer
be so, but let us determine to equal the whites among
whom we live, not by declarations and unexpressed
self-opinion, for we have always had enough of that,
but by actual proof in acting, doing, and carrying
out practically, the measures of equality. Here is
our nativity, and here have we the natural right to
abide and be elevated through the measures of our
own efforts.

CHAPTER VI.

THE UNITED STATES OUR COUNTRY.

OUR common country is the United States. Here
were we born, here raised and educated ; here are the
scenes of childhood; the pleasant associations of our
school going days; the loved enjoyments of our
domestic and fireside relations, and the sacred graves
of our departed fathers and mothers, and from here
will we not be driven by any policy that may be
schemed against us.

We are Americans, having a birthright citizenship
—natural claims upon the country—claims common

to all others of our fellow citizens—natural rights, which may, by virtue of unjust laws, be obstructed, but never can be annulled. Upon these do we place ourselves, as immovably fixed as the decrees of the living God. But according to the economy that regulates the policy of nations, upon which rests the basis of justifiable claims to all freemen's rights, it may be necessary to take another view of, and enquire into the political claims of colored men.

CHAPTER VII.

CLAIMS OF COLORED MEN AS CITIZENS OF THE UNITED STATES.

THE political basis upon which rests the establishment of all free nations, as the first act in their organization, is the security by constitutional provisions, of the fundamental claims of citizenship.

The legitimate requirement, politically considered, necessary to the justifiable claims for protection and full enjoyment of all the rights and privileges of an unqualified freeman, in all democratic countries is, that each person so endowed, shall have made contributions and investments in the country. Where there is no investment there can be but little interest; hence an adopted citizen is required to reside a sufficient length of time, to form an attachment and establish some interest in the country of his adoption, before he can rightfully lay any claims to citizenship. The pioneer who leads in the discovery or settlement of a country, as the first act to establish a right therein, erects a building of whatever dimensions, and seizes upon a portion of the soil. The soldier, who braves the dangers of the battle-field, in defence of his country's rights, and the toiling laborer and husband-man, who cuts down and removes the forest, levels and constructs post-roads and other public highways —the mechanic, who constructs and builds up houses, villages, towns, and cities, for the conveniency of inhabitants—the farmer, who cultivates the soil for the production of bread-stuffs and forage, as food and feed for man and beast—all of these are among the first people of a democratic state, whose claims are legitimate as freemen of the commonwealth. A free-man in a political sense, is a citizen of unrestricted rights in the state, being eligible to the highest position known to their civil code. They are the preferred persons in whom may be invested the highest privileges, and to whom may be entrusted fundamen-tally the most sacred rights of the country ; because, having made the greatest investments, they necessarily have the greatest interests ; and consequently, are the safest hands into which to place so high and sacred a trust. Their interest being the country's, and the interest of the country being the interest of the people ; therefore, the protection of their own interests necessarily protects the interests of the whole country and people. It is this simple but great principle of

primitive rights, that forms the fundamental basis of
citizenship in all free countries, and it is upon this
principle, that the rights of the colored man in this
country to citizenship are fixed.

The object of this volume is, to enlighten the
minds of a large class of readers upon a subject with
which they are unacquainted, expressed in comprehensible language, therefore we have studiously avoided
using political and legal phrases, that would serve
more to perplex than inform them. To talk about
the barons, king John, and the Magna Charta, would
be foreign to a work like this, and only destroy
the interest that otherwise might be elicited in the
subject. Our desire is, to arrest the attention of the
American people in general, and the colored people
in particular, to great truths as heretofore but little
thought of. What claims then have colored men,
based upon the principles set forth, as fundamentally
entitled to citizenship? Let the living records of
history answer the enquiry.

When Christopher Columbus, in 1492, discovered
America, natives were found to pay little or no attention to cultivation, being accustomed by hereditary
pursuit, to war, fishing, and the sports of the chase.
The Spaniards and Portuguese, as well as other Europeans who ventured here, came as mineral speculators,
and not for the purpose of improving the country.

As the first objects of speculation are the develope-
ments of the mineral wealth of every newly discovered country, so was it with this. Those who came
to the new world, were not of the common people,

seeking in a distant land the means of livelihood, but moneyed capitalists, the grandees and nobles, who reduced the natives to servitude by confining them to the mines. To have brought large numbers of the peasantry at that early period, from the monarchies of Europe, to the wilds of America, far distant fro the civil and military powers of the home governments, would have been to place the means of self-control into their own hands, and invite them to rebellion against the crowns. The capitalist miners were few, compared to the number of laborers required; and the difficulty at that time of the transportation of suitable provisions for their sustenance, conduced much to the objection of bringing them here. The natives were numerous, then easily approached by the wily seductions of the Europeans, easily yoked and supported, having the means of sustenance at hand, the wild fruits and game of the forest, the fish of the waters and birds of the country. All these as naturally enough, European adventurers would be cautious against introducing into common use among hundreds of thousands of laborers, under all the influences incident to a foreign climate in a foreign country, in its primitive natural state. The Indians were then preferred for many reasons, as the common laborers on the continent, where nothing but the mining interests were thought of or carried on. This noble race of Aborigines, continued as the common slaves of the new world, to bear the yoke of foreign oppression, until necessity induced a substitute for them. They sunk by scores under the heavy weight of oppression, and were fast passing from the shores of time. At this, the foreigners grew alarmed, and of necessity, devised ways and means to obtain an adequate substitute. A few European laborers were brought into the country, but the influence of climate and mode of living, operated entirely against them. They were as inadequate to stand the climate, as the nobles were themselves.

From the earliest period of the history of nations, the African race had been known as an industrious people, cultivators of the soil. The grain fields of Ethiopia and Egypt were the themes of the poet, and their garners, the subject of the historian. Like the present America, all the world went to Africa, to get a supply of commodities. Their massive piles of masonry, their skilful architecture, their subterranean vaults, their deep and mysterious wells, their extensive artificial channels, their mighty sculptured solid rocks, and provinces of stone quarries; gave indisputable evidence, of the hardihood of that race of people.

Nor was Africa then, without the evidence of industry, as history will testify. All travelers who had penetrated towards the interior of the continent, have been surprised at the seeming state of civilization and evidences of industry among the inhabitants of that vast country. These facts were familiar to Europeans, who were continually trading on coast of Africa, as it was then the most important part of adventure and research, known to the world. In later periods still, the history of African travelers, confirm all the former accounts concerning the industry of the people.

John and Richard Lander, two young English noblemen, in 1828, under the patronage of the English government, sailed to the western coast of Africa, on an expedition of research. In their voyage up the river Niger, their description of the scenes is extravagant. They represent the country on each side of the river, for several hundred miles up the valley, as being not only beautiful and picturesque, but the fields as in a high state of cultivation, clothed in the verdure of husbandry, waving before the gentle breezes, with the rich products of industry—maize, oats, rye, millet, and wheat, being among the fruits of cultivation. The fences were of various descriptions : hedge, wicker, some few pannel, and the old fashioned zigzag, known as the " Virginia worm fence"—the hedge and worm fence being the most common. Their cattle were fine and in good order, looking in every particular, except perhaps in size, as well as European cattle on the best managed farms. The fruit groves were delightful to the eye of the beholder. Every variety common to the country, were there to be seen in a high state of cultivation. Their roads and public highways were in good condition, and well laid out, as by the direction of skillful supervising surveyors. The villages, towns, and cities, many of them, being a credit to the people. Their cities were well laid out, and presented evidence of educated minds and mechanical ingenuity. In many of the workshops in which they went, they found skillful workmen, in iron, copper, brass, steel, and gold; and their implements of husbandry and war, were as well manufactured by African sons of toil, as any in the English manufactories, save that they had not quite so fine a finish, garnish and embellishment. This is a description, given of the industry and adaptedness of the people of Africa, to labor and toil of every kind. As it was very evident, that where there were manufactories of various metals, the people must of necessity be inured to mining operations, so it was also very evident, that this people must be a very hardy and enduring people.

In 1442, fifty years previous to the sailing of Columbus in search of a new world, Anthony Gonzales, Portuguese, took from the gold coast of Guinea, ten Africans and a quantity of gold dust, which he carried back to Lisbon with him. These Africans were set immediately to work in the gardens of the emperor, which so pleased his queen, that the number were much augmented, all of whom were found to be skillful and industrious in agriculture.

In 1481, eleven years prior to the discovery by Columbus, the Portuguese built a fort on the Gold Coast, and there commenced mining in search of gold. During this time until the year 1502, a period of ten years, had there been no other evidence, there was sufficient time and opportunity, to give full practical demonstrations of the capacity of this people to endure toil, especially in the mining operations, and for this cause and this alone, were they selected in preference to any other race of men, to do the labor of the New World. They had proven themselves physically

superior either to the European or American races—
in fact, superior physically to any living race of men
—enduring fatigue, hunger and thirst—enduring
change of climate, habits, manners and customs, with
infinitely far less injury to their physical and mental
system, than any other people on the face of God's
earth.

The following extract shows, that even up to the year 1676, the
Indians were enslaved—but that little value were attached to them as
laborers, as the price at which they were disposed and sold to purcha-
sers, fully shows :

SLAVERY IN PROVIDENCE, R. I.—Immediately after the struggle
between the natives and some of the New England settlers, known
as " King Philip's war," it became necessary to dispose of certain Indian captives then in Providence. The method adopted was common
in that day, but to us remarkable, as also the names of those who fig-
ured prominently therein. Only think of ROGER WILLIAMS sharing
in the proceeds of a slave sale. The following is from the " Annals
of Providence."

" A town meeting was held before Thomas Field's house, under a
tree, by the water side, on the 14th of August, 1676. A committee
was appointed to determine in what manner the Indians should be
disposed of. They reported as follows :

" Inhabitants wanting, can have Indians at the price they sell at
the Island of Rhode Island or elsewhere. All under five, to serve till
thirty ; above five and under ten, till twenty-eight ; above ten to fifteen, till twenty-seven ; above fifteen to twenty, till twenty-six ; from
twenty to thirty, shall serve eight years ; all above thirty, seven years.

" We whose names are underwritten, being chosen by the town to
see to the disposal of the Indians now in town, we agree that Roger
Williams, N. Waterman, T. Fenner, H. Ashton, J. Morey, D. Abbot,
J. Olney, V. Whitman, J. Whipple, sen., E. Pray, J. Pray, J. Angell, Jas. Angell, T. Arnold, A. Man, T. Field, E. Bennett, T. Clem-
ence, W. Lancaster, W. Hopkins, W. Hawkins, W. Harris, Z. Field,
S. Winsor, and Capt. Fenner, shall each have a whole share in the
product. I. Woodward and R. Pray, three-fourths of a share each.

J. Smith, E. Smith, S. Whipple, N. Whipple and T. Walling each half a share."

Signed, " Roger Williams, Thomas Harris, sen., Thomas [⋈] Angell, Thomas Field, John Whipple, Jr."

To gratify curiosity as to the price of Indians on those terms, the following extracts are made from an account of sales about this time;

" To Anthony Low, five Indians, great and small, £8.

" To James Rogers, two, for twenty bushels of Indian corn.

" To Philip Smith, two, in silver, $4 10.

" To Daniel Allen, one, in silver, $2 10.

" To C. Carr, one, twelve bushels of Indian corn.

" To Elisha Smith, one, in wool, 100 lbs.

" To   "   "   one, for three fat sheep."

From 1492, the discovery of Hispaniola, to 1502, the short space of but four years, such was the mortality among the natives, that the Spaniards then holding rule there, " began to employ a few" Africans in the mines of the Island. The experiment was effective—a successful one. The Indian and African were enslaved together, when the Indian sunk, and the African stood. It was not until June the 24th of the year 1498, that the Continent was discovered by John Cabot, a Venitian, who sailed in August of the previous year 1497, from Bristol, under the patronage of Henry VII., King of England, with two vessels " freighted by the merchants of London and Bristol, with articles of traffic," his son Sebastian, and 300 men. In 1517, but the short period of thirteen years from the date of their first introduction, Carolus V., King of Spain, by the right of a patent, granted permission to a number of persons, annually, to supply to the Islands of Hispaniola, (St. Domingo,) Cuba, Jamaica, and Porto Rico, natives of Africa, to the number of four thousand annually. John Hawkins, an unprincipled Englishman—whose name should be branded with infamy—was the first person known to have engaged in so inhuman a traffic, and that living monster his mistress, Queen Elizabeth, engaged with him and shared in the profits.

The natives of Africa, on their introduction into a foreign country, soon discovered the loss of their accustomed food, and mode and manner of living. The Aborigines subsisted mainly by game and fish, with a few patches of maize or Indian corn near their wigwams, which were generally attended by the women, while the men were absent. The grains and fruits, such as they had been accustomed to, were not to be had among the Aborigines of the country, and this first induced the African to cultivate patches of ground in the neighborhood of the mines, for the raising of food for his own sustenance. This trait in their character was observed, and regarded by the Spaniards with considerable interest; and when on contracting with the English slave-dealer, Captain Hawkins, and others for new supplies of slaves, they were careful to request them to secure a quantity of the seeds and different products of the country, to bring with them to the New World. Many of these were cultivated to some extent, while those indigenous to America, were cultivated by them with considerable success. And up to this day, it is a custom on many of the slave plantations of the South, to allow the slave his "patch," and Saturday afternoon or Sabbath day, to cultivate it.

Shortly after the commencement of the shameful traffic in the blood and bones of men—the destiny and chastity of women by Captain Hawkins, and what was termed England's "Virgin Queen;" Elizabeth gave a license to Sir Walter Raleigh, to search for uninhabited lands, and seize upon all uninhabited by Christians. Sir Walter discovered the coast of North Carolina and Virginia, assigning the name of "Virginia" to the whole coast now composing the old state. A feeble colony was settled here, which did not avail, and it was not until the month of April, 1607, that the first permanent settlement was made in Virginia, under the patronage of letters patent from James I., King of England, to Thomas Gates and his associates.

This was the first settling of North America, and thirteen years anterior to the landing of the Pilgrims.

"No permanent settlement was effected in what is now called the United States, till the reign of James the First."—Ramsay's Hist. U. S., vol. I., p. 38.

"The month of April, 1607, is the epoch òf the first permanent settlement on the coast of Virginia; the name then given to all that extent of country which forms thirteen States."—Ib. p. 39. The whole coast of the country was now explored, not for the purpose of trade and agriculture—because there were no products in the country—the natives not producing sufficient provisions to supply present wants, and, consequently, nothing to trade for; but like the speculations of their Spanish and Portuguese predecessors, on

the islands and in South America, but for that of mining gold. Trade and the cultivation of the soil was
foreign to their designs and intention on coming to
the continent of the new world, and they were consequently, disappointed when failing of success. "At a
time when the precious metals were conceived to be
the peculiar and only valuable productions of the new
world, when every mountain was supposed to contain
a treasure, and every rivulet was searched for its
golden sands, this appearance was fondly considered as
an infallible indication of the mine. Every hand was
eager to dig."   *   *   *

"There was now," says Smith, "no talk, no hope,
no work; but dig gold, wash gold, refine gold. With
this imaginary wealth, the first vessel returning to
England was loaded, while the *culture of the land*, and
every useful occupation was *totally neglected.*" * * *

The colonists, thus left, were in miserable circumstances for want of provisions. The remainder of
what they had brought with them, was so small in
quantity, as to be soon expended—and so damaged in
the course of a long voyage, as to be a source of disease. * * * In their expectation of getting gold,
the people were disappointed, the glittering substance
they had sent to England, proving to be a valueless
mineral. "Smith, on his return to Jamestown, found
the colony reduced to thirty-eight persons, who, in
despair, were preparing to abandon the country. He
employed caresses, threats, and even violence, in order
to prevent them from executing this fatal resolution."
Ibid., pp. 45–6. In November, 1620, the Pilgrims

or Puritans made the harbor of Cape Cod, and after solemn vows and organization previous to setting foot on shore, they landed safely on "Plymouth Rock," December the 20th, about one month after. They were one hundred and one in number, and from the toils and hardships consequent to a severe season, in a strange country, in less than six months after their arrival, "forty-four persons, nearly one-half of their original number," had died.

    *   *   * "In 1618, in the reign of James I., the British government established a regular trade on the coast of Africa. In the year 1620, negro slaves began to be imported into Virginia: a Dutch ship bringing twenty of them for sale."—Sampson's Hist. Dict., p. 348. The Dutch ship landed her cargo at New Bedford, (now Massachusetts,) as it will be remembered, that the whole coast, now comprising the "Old Thirteen," and original United States, was then called Virginia, so named by Sir Walter Raleigh, in honor of his royal Mistress and patron, Elizabeth, the Virgin Queen, under whom he received his royal patent commission of adventure and expedition.

Beginning their preparation in the slave-trade in 1618, just two years previous, giving time for successfully carrying out the project against the landing of the first emigrant settlers, it will be observed that the African captain, and the "Puritan" emigrants, landed upon the same section of the continent at the same time, 1620—the Pilgrims at Plymouth, and the captives at New Bedford, but a few miles comparatively south.

The country at this period, was one vast wilderness.
"The continent of North America was then one continued forest."   *   *   *   There were no horses,
cattle, sheep, hogs, or tame beasts of any kind. * * *
There were no domestic poultry.   *   *   *   There
were no gardens, orchards, public roads, meadows, or
cultivated fields.   *   *   *   They " often burned the
woods that they could advantageously plant their
corn."   *   *   *   They had neither spice, salt, bread,
butter, cheese, nor milk.   *   *   *   They had no set
meals, but eat when they were hungry, and could find
any thing to satisfy the cravings of nature.   *   *   *
Very little of their food was derived from the earth,
except what it spontaneously produced.   *   *   *
The ground was both their seat and table.   *   *   *
Their best bed was a skin.   *   *   *   They had
neither steel, iron, nor any metallic instruments.
*   *   *—Ramsay's Hist., pp. 39–40.

    We adduce not these historical extracts to disparage
our brother the Indian—far be it: whatever he may
think of our race, according to the manner in which
he has been instructed to look upon it, by our mutual
oppressor the American nation; we admire his, for
the many deeds of noble daring, for which the short
history of his liberty-loving people are replete: we
sympathise with them, because our brethren are the
successors of their fathers in the degradation of American bondage—but we adduce them in evidence against
the many aspersions charged against the African
race, that their inferiority to the other races caused
them to be reduced to servitude.   For the purpose of

proving that their superiority, and not inferiority, alone was the cause which first suggested to Europeans the substitution of Africans for that of aboriginal or Indian laborers in the mines; and that their superior skill and industry, first suggested to the colonists, the propriety of turning their attention to agricultural and other industrial pursuits, than that of mining.

It is very evident, from what has been adduced, the settlement of Captain John Smith, being in the course of a few months, reduced to thirty-eight, and that of Plymouth, from one hundred and one, to that of fifty-seven in six months—it is evident, that the whites nor the Indians were equal to the hard and almost insurmountable difficulties, that now stood wide-spread before them.

An endless forest, the impenetrable earth; the one to be removed, and the other to be excavated. Towns and cities to be built, and farms to be cutivated—all these presented difficulties too arduous for the European then here, and unknown to the Indian.

It is very evident, that at a period such as this, when the natives themselves had fallen victims to tasks imposed upon them by their usurpers, and the Europeans were sinking beneath the weight of climate and hardships; when food could not be had nor the common conveniences of life procured—when arduous duties of life were to be performed and none capable of doing them, but those who had previously by their labors, not only in their native country, but in the new, so proven themselves—as the most natural consequence, the Africans were resorted to, for the performance of every duty common to domestic life.

There were no laborers known to the colonists from Cape Cod to Cape Look Out, than those of the African race. They entered at once into the mines, extracting therefrom, the rich treasures that for a thousand ages lay hidden in the earth. And from their knowledge of cultivation, the farming interests in the North, and planting in the South, were commenced with a prospect never dreamed of before the introduction of this most extraordinary, hardy race of men: though pagans, yet skilled in all the useful duties of life. Farmers, herdsmen, and laborers in their own country, they required not to be taught to work, and how to do it—but it was only necessary to tell them to go to work, and they at once knew what to do, and how it should be done.

It is notorious, that in the planting States, the blacks themselves are the only skillful cultivators— the proprietor knowing little or nothing about the art, save that which he learns. from the African husbandman, while his ignorant white overseer, who is merely there to see that the work is attended to, knows a great deal less. Tobacco, cotton, rice, hemp, indigo, the improvement in Indian corn, and many other important products, are all the result of African skill and labor in this country. And the introduction of the zigzag, or " Virginia Worm Fence," is purely of African origin. Nor was their skill as herdsmen inferior to their other attainments, being among the most accomplished trainers and horsemen in the world. Indeed, to this class of men may be indebted the entire country for the improvement South in the breed of horses. And any one who has travelled South, could not fail to have observed, that all of the leading trainers, jockies, and judges of horses, as well as riders, are men of African descent.

In speaking of the Bornouese, a people from among whom a great many natives have been enslaved by Arabian traders, and sold into foreign bondage, and of course many into this country, " It is said that Bornou can muster 15,000 Shonaas in the field mounted. They are the greatest breeders of cattle in the country, and annually supply Soudan with from two to three thousand horses." * * *

" Our road lying along one of them, gave me an excellent view of beautiful villages all round, and herds of cattle grazing in the open country." * *

" Plantations of cotton or indigo now occupy the place where the houses formerly stood." * * *

" The Souga market is well supplied with every necessary and luxury in request among the people of the interior." " The country still open and well cultivated, and the villages numerous. We met crowds of people coming from Karro with goods. Some carried them on their heads, others had asses or bullocks, according to their wealth." * * *

" The country still highly cultivated." * * *

" We also passed several walled towns, quite deserted, the inhabitants having been sold by their conquerors, the Felatohs." " Women sat spinning cotton by the road side, offering for sale to the passing caravans,

gussub water, roast-meat, sweet potatoes, coshen
nuts," &c. (Dunham and Clapperton's Travels and
Discoveries in North and Central Africa. Vol. 2,
pp. 140. 230. 332, 333. 353.)

The forests gave way before them, and extensive
verdant fields, richly clothed with produce, rose up as
by magic before these hardy sons of toil.   In the
place of the unskillful and ill-constructed wigwam,
houses, villages, towns and cities quickly were reared
up in their stead. Being farmers, mechanics, laborers
and traders in their own country, they required little
or no instruction in these various pursuits.   They
were in fact, then, to the whole continent, what they
are in truth now to the whole Southern section of the
Union—the bone and sinews of the country.   And
even now, the existence of the white man, South,
depends entirely on the labor of the black man—the
idleness of the one, is sustained by the industry of
the other.   Public roads and highways are the result
of their labor, as are also the first public works, as
wharves, docks, forts, and all such improvements.
Are not these legitimate investments in the common
stock of the nation, which should command a proportionate interest?

We shall next proceed to review the contributions
of colored men to other departments of the nation,
and as among the most notorious and historical, we
refer to colored American warriors.

CHAPTER VIII.

COLORED AMERICAN WARRIORS.

AMONG the highest claims that an inhabitant has upon his country, is that of serving in its cause, and assisting to fight its battles. There is no responsibility attended with more personal hazard, and consequently, none for which the country owes a greater debt of gratitude. *Amor patria*, or love of country, is the first requisition and highest attribute of every citizen; and he who voluntarily ventures his own safety for that of his country, is a patriot of the purest character.

When the country's attention is arrested—her fears aroused—her peace disturbed, and her independence endangered—when in the dread and momentous hour, the tap of the drum, the roll of the reveille, the shrill sound of the bugler's trumpet, or the thunders of the cannon's roar, summons the warrior on to the pending conflict—upon whom then do the citizens place their dependence, and in whom the country her trust? Upon him who braves the consequences, and fights his country's battles for his country's sake. Upon whom does the country look, as the most eligible of her favored sons? Upon none more so than he, who shoulders his musket, girds on his sword, and faces the enemy on to the charge. The hero and the warrior, have long been estimated, the favorite sons of a favored people.

In the Convention for the formation of the national compact, when the question arose on the priority of citizen's rights, an honorable member—Mr. Jefferson, if we mistake not—arose and stated, that for the purpose of henceforward settling a question of such moment to the American people, that nativity of birth, and the descendants of all who had borne arms in their country's struggle for liberty, should be always entitled to all the rights and privileges to which an American citizen could be eligible. This at once, enfranchised the native citizen, and the posterity of all those at the time, who may have been so fortunate as to have been born on the American continent. The question was at once settled, as regards American citizenship. And if we establish our right of equal claims to citizenship with other American people, we shall have done all that is desirable in this view of our position in the country. But if in addition to this, we shall be able to prove, that colored men, not only took part in the great scene of the first act for independence, but that they were the actors—a colored man was really the hero in the great drama, and actually the first victim in the revolutionary tragedy—then indeed, shall we have more than succeeded, and have reared a monument of fame to the history of our deeds, more lasting than the pile that stands on Bunker Hill.

For a concise historical arrangement of colored men, who braved the dangers of the battlefield, we

are much indebted to William C. Nell, Esq., formerly
of Boston, now of Rochester, N. Y., for a pamphlet,
published by him during the last year, which should
be read by every American the country through.

For ten years previous, a dissatisfaction had pre-
vailed among the colonists, against the mother country, in consequence of the excessive draughts of supplies, and taxation, made upon them, for the support
of the wars carried on in Europe. The aspect began
to change, the light grew dim, the sky darkened, the
clouds gathered lower and lower, the lightning glim-
mered through the black elements around—the storm
advanced, until on the fifth of March, 1773, it broke
out in terrible blasts, drenching the virgin soil of
America, with the blood of her own native sons—
Crispus Attuck, a colored man, was the first who
headed, the first who commanded, the first who
charged, who struck the first blow, and the first whose
blood was spilt, and baptized the colony, as a peace-
offering on the altar of American liberty. "The
people were greatly exasperated. The multitude,
armed with clubs, ran towards King street, crying,
'Let us drive out the ribalds; they have no business
here!' The rioters rushed furiously towards the Custom House; they approached the sentinel crying,
'Kill him, kill him!' They assaulted him with snow-
balls, pieces of ice, and whatever they could lay their
hands upon. They encountered a band of the populace led by a mulatto named Attucks, who brandished
their clubs and pelted them with snow-balls. The
maledictions, the imprecations, the execrations of the

multitude were horrible.   In the midst of a torrent of
invectives from every quarter, the military were chal-
lenged to fire. The populace advanced to the points of
the bayonets : the soldiers appeared like statues ; the
cries, the howlings, the menaces, the violent din of bells
still sounding the alarm, increased the confusion and the
horrors of these moments : at length the mulatto and
twelve of his companions, pressing forward environed
the soldiers, and striking their muskets with their clubs
cried to the multitude : ' Be not afraid, they dare not
fire ; why do you hesitate, why do you not kill them,
why not crush them at once ?' The mulatto lifted his
arm against Captain Preston, having turned one of the
muskets, he seized the bayonet with his left hand, as
if he intended to execute his threat.   At this moment confused cries were heard : ' The wretches dare
not fire !' Firing succeeds. Attucks is slain. Two
other discharges follow. Three were killed, five se-
verely wounded, and several others slightly."   Attucks was killed by Montgomery, one of Captain
Preston's soldiers. He had been foremost in resisting,
and was first slain ; as proof of front and close engagement, received two balls, one in each breast."
" John Adams, counsel for the soldier, admitted that
Attucks appeared to have undertaken to be the hero
of the night, and to lead the army with banners. John
Hancock, in 1774, invokes the injured shades of Maver-
ick, Gray, Caldwell, *Attucks* and Carr." *Nell's Wars,*
1776 and 1812, pp. 5, 6.—RHODE ISLAND also contributes largely to the capital stock of citizenship. " In
Rhode Island, the blacks formed an entire regiment,

and they discharged their duty with zeal and fidelity. The gallant defence of Red Bank, in which the black regiment bore a part, is among the proofs of their valor." In this contest it will be recollected, that four hundred men met and repulsed, after a terrible sanguinary struggle, fifteen hundred Hessian troops, headed by count Donop." *Ibid.* p. 10. CONNECTICUT next claims to be heard and given credit on the nation's books. In speaking of the patriots who bore the standard of their country's glory, Judge Goddard, who held the office of commissioner of pensions for nineteen colored soldiers, says, " I cannot refrain from mentioning one aged black man, Primus Babcock, who proudly presented to me an honorable discharge from service during the war, dated at the close of it, wholly in the hand-writing of GEORGE WASHINGTON. Nor can I forget the expression of his feelings, when informed that, after his discharge had been sent to the department, that it could not be returned. At his request it was written for, as he seemed to spurn the pension and reclaim the discharge." It is related of Babcock, that when the British in a successful charge took a number of the Americans prisoners, they were ordered to deliver up their arms by the British officer of the detachment, which demand was readily conceded to by all the prisoners except Babcock, who looking at the officer sternly —at the margin of a mud pond foot of Bunker Hill —turned his musket bayonet downwards, thrusting it into the mire up to the armpit, drawing out his muddy arm, turned to the British officer, and said, " Now

dirty your silk glove, and take it—you red coat!"
The officer raised his sword as if to cut him down for
the impertinence, then replied, "You are too brave a
soldier to be killed, you black devil!" A few years
since, a musket evidently a relic of the Revolution,
was found near the same spot in the singular position
of that thrust down by Babcock, no doubt being the
same, which was deposited among the relics in the
archives at Washington. Babcock died but a few
years ago, aged we believe 101 years.

"When Major Montgomery, one of the leaders in
the expedition against the colonists, was lifted upon
the walls of the fort by his soldiers, flourishing his
sword and calling on them to follow him, Jordan Freeman received him on the point of a pike and pinned
him dead to the earth." "NEW HAMPSHIRE gives her
testimony to the deposit of colored interest. There
was a regiment of blacks in the same situation, a regiment of negroes fighting for our liberty and independence, not a white man among them but the officers,
in the same dangerous and responsible position. Had
they been unfaithful, or given way before the enemy
all would have been lost. Three times in succession
were they attacked with most desperate fury by well
disciplined and veteran troops, and three times did
they successfully repel the assault, and thus preserve
the army. They fought thus through the war. They
were brave and hearty troops." *Nell*, pp. 11, 13.

NEW YORK comes bravely to the call, and sends her
investments by land and sea. In the convention of
1821, for revising the constitution of the State, the

question of equal rights having been introduced, Doctor Clarke among other things said, "In the war of
the Revolution, these people helped to fight our battles by land and by sea. Some of your states were
glad to turn out corps of colored men, and to stand
'shoulder to shoulder' with them. In your late war,
they contributed largely towards some of your most
splendid victories. On lakes Erie and Champlain,
where your fleets triumphed over a foe superior in
numbers and engines of death, they were manned in
a large proportion with men of color. And in this
very house, in the fall of 1814, a bill passed receiving
all the branches of your government, authorising the
governor to accept the services of a corps of two
thousand free people of color. These were times
when a man who shouldered his musket did not know
but he bared his bosom to receive a death wound from
the enemy ere he laid it aside; and in these times
these people were found as ready and as willing to
volunteer in your service as any other. They were
not compelled to go; they were not draughted.* * They
were volunteers.* * Said Martindale of New York in
congress 22 of first month 1828: "Slaves, or negroes
who had been slaves, were enlisted as soldiers in the
War of the Revolution; and I myself saw a battalion
of them, as fine martial looking men as I ever saw,
attached to the northern army in the last war, on its
march from Plattsburg to Sackett's Harbor."

PENNSYLVANIA contributes an important share in
the stock of Independence, as will be seen by the following historical reminiscence: "On the capture of

Washington by the British forces, it was judged expedient to fortify without delay, the principal towns and cities exposed to similar attacks. The Vigilance Committee of Philadelphia waited upon three of the principal Colored citizens, namely, James Forten, Bishop Allen, and Absalom Jones, soliciting the aid of the people of Color in erecting suitable defences for the city. Accordingly two thousand five hundred Colored men assembled in the State House yard, and from thence marched to Gray's Ferry, where they labored for two days, almost without intermission. Their labors were so faithful and efficient, that a vote of thanks was tendered them by the Committee. A battalion of Colored troops were at the same time organized in the city, under an officer of the United States army ; and they were on the point of marching to the fron-. tier when peace was proclaimed."—*Ibid.* pp. 14–17–18.*

* Captain Jonathan Tudas, who led the 500 brave blacks out to build the Redoubt, is now living in Philadelphia, and since the commencement of this publication, we learned the following particulars : When the news arrived of the approach of the British under Major General Ross, upon Baltimore, the expectation ran high, that the city would be taken, and forced marches made, immediately upon Philadelphia. The whole City consequently was thrown into great alarm, when Captain Tudas, applied to the United States Engineer, and offered the services of colored men, who during the week, were summoned to meet at the African Methodist Episcopal Church, on the following Sabbath ; when from the pulpit, the Right Rev. Richard Allen, Bishop of the Connexion, made known to the people the peril of the Country, and demands of the Commonwealth ; when, the next day, Monday, five hundred volunteered, working incessantly during that day, and on Tuesday, six hundred more were added, swelling the

And even in the slave States, where might reasonably be expected, nothing but bitter hate and burning
revenge to exist—where the displeasure of Heaven
and anger of God was invoked—where it is thought
the last glimmering spark of patriotic fire has been
quenched, and every aid withheld—even there, in the
hour of their country's danger, did they lay aside every consideration of the ten thousand wrongs inflicted
—throw in their contributions, and make common
cause.

Says Mr. Nell, "The celebrated Charles Pinkney,
of South Carolina, in his speech on the Missouri question, in defence of the Slave representation of the
South, made the following admission :—They (the colored people) were in numerous instances the pioneers,

number to eleven hundred men. William Stansberry, arrested and
tried a few years ago, as a fugitive slave from Maryland, and Mr.
Ignatius Beck, an old respectable colored man, who appeared as a
witness, and by whose testimony alone, Mr. Stansberry was released
from the grasp of the oppression of his Country, and thereby saved
from endless bondage, were both under Captain Tudas, and belong to
the faithful eleven hundred Philadelphia black warriors. He farther
informs us, that the Engineer gave them credit for having thrown up
superior works to any other men employed in the service, and having
done more work in the same time, and *drank less*, by four-fifth, than
twice their number of " Old Countrymen." The relics of the breast-
works, still stand on or near the banks of the Schuylkill, as a living
monument of the fidelity of the black race to their State and Country.
Mr. Stansberry, is still living, and Captain Tudas, now quite an old
man, about "turning the corner," as he expresses it, is a very intelligent old gentleman, and a living history of facts. There are few
white men of his age and opportunities, that equal him at all in intelligence on any subject. He is a kind of living synoptic-historical
Encyclopædia.

an⌣ ⌐ all the labors of our army. To their hands
we are owing the greatest part of the fortifications
raised for the protection of the country. Fort Moul-
trie gave, at an early period of inexperience and un-
tried valor of our citizens, immortality to the American
arms." And were there no other proof on record, the
testimony given to the brave followers of the renowned
hero of Chalmet Plains, would of itself be sufficient to
establish the right of the colored man to eligibility in
his native country. " In 1814," continues Mr. Nell,
" when New Orleans was in danger, and the proud
criminal distinctions of caste were again demolished
by one of those emergencies in which nature puts to
silence for the moment the base partialities of art, the
free colored people were called into the field in common with the whites; and the importance of their services was thus acknowledged by General Jackson :—

" HEAD-QUARTERS, SEVENTH MILITARY DIS-
TRICT, MOBILE, SEPTEMBER 21, 1814.
" *To the Free Colored Inhabitants of Louisiana :*
" Through a mistaken policy, you have heretofore
been deprived of a participation in the glorious struggle for national rights, in which *our* country is engaged. This no longer shall exist. As sons of Freedom you are now called upon to defend your most
estimable blessings. *As Americans,* your country
looks with confidence to her adopted children, for a
valorous support, as a faithful return for the advantages enjoyed under her mild and equitable government. As fathers, husbands, and brothers, you are

summoned to rally round the standard of the Eagle, to defend all which is dear in existence.

" *Your country*, although calling for your exertions, does not wish you to engage in her cause, without remunerating you for the services rendered. Your intelligent minds are not to be led away by false representations—your love of honor would cause you to despise the man who should attempt to deceive you. In the sincerity of a soldier, and the language of truth I address you.

" To every noble hearted free man of color, volunteering to serve during the present contest with Great Britain, and no longer, there will be paid the same bounty in money and lands now received by white soldiers of the United States, namely, one hundred and twenty-four dollars in money and one hundred and sixty acres in land. The non-commissioned officers and privates will also be entitled to the same monthly pay and daily rations and clothes furnished to any American soldiers.

" On enrolling yourselves in companies, the Major General commanding will select officers for your government from your white fellow-citizens. Your non-commissioned officers will be appointed from among yourselves.

" Due regard will be paid to the feelings of free men and soldiers.

" You will not, by being associated with white men in the same corps, be exposed to improper comparison, or unjust sarcasm. As a distinct, independent battalion or regiment, pursuing the path of glory, you will, undivided, receive the applause and gratitude of your countrymen.

"To assure you of the sincerity of my intentions, and my anxiety to engage your invaluable services to our country, I have communicated my wish to the Governor of Louisiana, who is fully informed as to the manner of enrollments, and will give you every necessary information on the subject of this address.

"ANDREW JACKSON,
"Major General Commanding."

On the 18th of December, 1814, through his Aid-de-camp, Colonel Butler, the General issued another address to the colored soldiers, who had proven themselves, in every particular, worthy of their country's trust, and in every way worthy of the proudest position of enfranchised freemen. To deny to men and their descendants, who are capable of such deeds as are acknowledged in this proclamation, equal rights with other men, is a moral homicide—an assassination, which none but the most malicious and obdurate are capable of perpetrating. Surely, surely, it cannot be, that our fellow-citizens, who control the destiny of the country, one fully advised of the claims of their brethren in adversity—we cannot be persuaded that a people, claiming the self-respect and consideration of the American people, can be satisfied that the perils of war be encountered by them—their country's rights sustained—and their liberty, the liberty of their wives and children defended and protected; then, with a cool deliberation, unknown to any un-civilized people on the face of the earth, deny them a

right—withhold their consent to their having equal
enjoyment of human rights with other citizens, with
those who have never contributed aid to our country—
but we give the proclamation and let it speak for
itself. Of it Mr. Nell says:—

"The second proclamation is one of the highest
compliments ever paid by a military chief to his soldiers."

"SOLDIERS! When on the banks of the Mobile, I
called you to take up arms, inviting you to partake
the perils and glory of your *white fellow-citizens, I
expected much* from you; for I was not ignorant that
you possessed qualities most formidable to an invad-
ing enemy. I knew with what fortitude you could
endure hunger and thirst, and all the fatigues of
a campaign. *I knew well how you love your native country*, and that you, as well as ourselves, had to
defend what *man* holds most dear—his parents, wife,
children, and property. *You have done more than I
expected.* In addition to the previous qualities I before knew you to possess, I found among you noble
enthusiasm, which leads to the performance of great
things.

"Soldiers! The President of the United States
shall hear how praise-worthy was your conduct in the
hour of danger; and the representatives of the American people will give you the praise your exploits entitle you to. The General anticipates them in ap-
plauding your noble ardor.

"The enemy approaches; his vessels cover our
lakes; our brave citizens are united, and all conten-

tions have ceased among them. Their only dispute is, who shall win the prize of valor, or who the most glory, its noblest reward.

"By order,
'THOMAS BUTLER, Aid-de-camp."

A circumstance that reflects as well upon the devisor, as upon the commander, or the engineer of the army, is not generally known to the American people. The redoubt of cotton bales, has ever been attributed to the judgment, skill, quick perception, and superior tact of Major General Andrew Jackson; than whom, a braver heart, never beat in the breast of man. But this is a mistake. The suggestion of the cotton bales was made by a colored man, at the instant, when the city of New Orleans was put under martial law. The colored troops were gathering, and their recruiting officers (being colored,) were scouring the city in every direction, and particularly on the Levee, where the people throng for news—to hear, see, and be seen. At such times in particular, the blacks are found in great numbers. The cotton shipped down the Mississippi in large quantities to the city, is landed and piled in regular terrace walls, several thousand feet long, sometimes double rows—and fifteen or twenty feet high. When the sun shines in winter, the days become warm and pleasant after the morning passes off, and at such times, there may be found many of the idle blacks, lying upon the top, and in comfortable positions between or behind those walls of cotton bales. On the approach of the recruiting officer, a number of persons were found stretched out upon the bales, lying scattered upon the ground. On addressing them, they were found to be slaves, which the pride of the recently promoted free colored soldiers, nor the policy of the proclamation, then, justified them in enrolling. On questioning them respecting their fears of the approaching contest—they expressed themselves as perfectly satisfied and *safe*, while permitted to lie *behind* the bales. The idea was at once impressed— Chalmet Plain, the battle field, being entirely barren without trees, brush, or stone, and the ingenuity of the General-in-chief and engineer of the army, having been for several days taxed, without successful device; the officer determined that he would muster courage, and hazard the consequences of an approach to the General, and suggest the idea suggested to him, by the observation of a slave, who was indifferent to the safety of others, so that he was secure—and perhaps justly so—whether conscious or not of the importance of its bearing. General Jackson, whatever may be said to the contrary, though firm and determined, was pleasant, affable, and easily approached, and always set equal estimate upon the manhood of a colored man ; believing every thing of him, that he expressed in his proclamation to the colored freemen of Louisiana. He did not pretend to justify the holding of slaves, especially on the assumed unjust plea of their incapacity for self-government—he always hooted at the idea ; never would become a member of the Colonization Society, always saying " Let the colored people be—they were quiet now, in comparative satisfaction—let them be." But he held them as a policy,

by which to make money—and would just as readily
have held a white man, had it been the policy of the
country, as a black one in slavery. The General was
approached—the suggestion made—slaves set to work
—the bales conveyed down—the breast-works raised
—the Americans protected, as the musketry and artil-
lery proved powerless against the elastic cushion-wall
of cotton bales; the battle fought—the British van-
quished—the Americans victorious, and Major General Andrew Jackson "all covered with glory," as the
most distinguished and skillful captain of the age. It
has always been thought by colored men familiar with
this circumstance, that the reference of the General
is directed to this, when he expresses himself in his
last proclamation to them: "*You have done more
than I expected.*" Doubtless this was the case. Whatever valor and capacity to endure hardships, the General knew colored men to possess, it *was* more than he
expected of them, to bring skill to his aid, and assist
in counseling plans for the defence of the army

On the *Eighth* of January, 1851, the celebration
of the Battle of New Orleans, in that city one year
ago, "Ninety of the colored veterans who bore a
conspicuous part in the dangers of the day," (the day
of battle,) held "a conspicuous place in the proces-
sion," in exaltation of their country's glory. Nor
was the

NAVY without the representative of colored interest
in the liberty of the country. In speaking of the
war of 1812, a colored veteran of Philadelphia, the
late James Forten, who had himself enlisted and was

imprisoned on board of a British man-of-war, the
" Old Jersey Prison Ship," affirms : " The vessels of
war of that period were all, to a greater or less extent,
manned with colored men." The father-in-law of
the writer, has often related to him that he saw the
three hundred and sixty colored marines, in military
pomp and naval array, when passing through Pittsburg in 1812 on their way to the frigate Constitution,
then on lake Erie under command of the gallant
Commodore Perry. And we cannot close this view
of our subject, without reference to one of the living
veterans of the battle of New Orleans, now residing
where he has for many years, in the city of Pittsburg,
Pa., to whom we are indebted for more oral information concerning that memorable conflict, than to any
other living person. MR. JOHN JULIUS, was a member of the valiant regiment of colored soldiers, who
held so conspicuous a place in the estimation of their
General, their country's struggles for Liberty and
Independence. He is a tall, good-looking, brown
skin creole of Louisiana, now about sixty-three years
of age, bearing the terrible gashes of the bayonet still
conspicuously in his neck. He was one of the few
Americans who encountered the British in single-
handed charges on the top of the breast-works.
Julien Bennoit, (pronounced *ben wah*,) for such is
his name, though commonly known as John Julius, is
a man of uprightness and strict integrity of character,
having all the delicate sensibility and pride of character known to the Frenchman ; and laments more at
the injustice done him, in the neglect of the authorities

to grant him his claims of money and land, according to the promises set forth in the Proclamation, than at any reverse of fortune with which he has ever met. He is enthusiastic on the subject of the battle scenes of Chalmet Plains, and anxious that all who converse with him may know that he is one of the actors. Not so much for his own notoriety—as all soldiers have a right to—as for the purpose of making known and exposing the wrongs done to him and hundreds of his fellows, who fought shoulder to shoulder with him, in the conflict with Sir Edward Packenham. Mr. Julius is the only person in whose possession we have ever seen a complete draught of the plan of the battle fought on the 8th of January, 1815, drawn on the field, by the U. S. Engineer.

This consists of two charts, one quite large, and the other smaller; the larger giving the whole plan of battle, and the other being the key, which shows the position of the different battalions and regiments of troops, with the several officers of command, in which the Colored Regiment is beautifully and conspicuously displayed. He sets great estimate upon them. Col. Marshall John M. Davis, who was an officer under General Jackson at the battle of New Orleans, now still residing in Alleghany Co., near Pittsburg, bears testimony to the truthfulness of Mr. Julien Bennoit having been a soldier in the Army of the Mississippi in 1814. The deeds of these tried and faithful daring sons of Liberty, and defenders of their country, shall live triumphantly, long after the nation shall have repented her wrongs towards them

and their descendants, and hung her head with shame,
before the gaze of manhood's stern rebuke.

Mr. John B. Vashon, of Pittsburg, embarked in the
service of the United States, and in an engagement
of the American squadron in South America, was
imprisoned, with Major Henry Bears, a respectable
white citizen, still living in that city.

———◦•◦———

CHAPTER IX.

CAPACITY OF COLORED MEN AND WOMEN AS CITIZEN MEMBERS OF COMMUNITY.

THE utility of men in their private capacity as citizens, is of no less import than that of any other department of the community in which they live ; indeed, the
fitness of men for positions in the body politic, can only be justly measured by their qualification as citizens.
And we may safely venture the declaration, that in the
history of the world, there has never been a nation,
that among the oppressed class of inhabitants—a class
entirely ineligible to any political position of honor,
profit or trust—wholly discarded from the recognition
of citizens' rights—not even permitted to carry the
mail, nor drive a mail coach—there never has, in the
history of nations, been any people thus situated, who
has made equal progress in attainments with the col-

ored people of the United States. It would be as un-
necessary as it is impossible, to particularize all the
individuals; we shall therefore be satisfied, with a
classification and a few individual cases. Our history
in this country is well known, and quite sufficiently
treated on in these pages already, without the necessity of repetition here; it is enough to know that by
the most cruel acts of injustice and crime, our forefathers were forced by small numbers, and enslaved
in the country—the great body now to the number of
three millions and a half, still groaning in bondage—
that the half million now free, are the descendants of
the few who by various means, are fortunate enough
to gain their liberty from Southern bondage—that no
act of general emancipation has ever taken place, and
no chance as yet for a general rebellion—we say in
view of all these facts, we proceed to give a cursory
history of the attainments—the civil, social, business
and professional, and literary attainments of colored
men and women, and challenge comparison with the
world—according to circumstances—in times past and
present.

Though shorn of their strength, disarmed of manhood, and stripped of every right, encouraged by the
part performed by their brethren and fathers in the
Revolutionary struggle—with no records of their
deeds in history, and no means of knowing them save
orally, as overheard from the mouths of their oppressors, and tradition as kept up among themselves—that
memorable event, had not yet ceased its thrill through
the new-born nation, until a glimmer of hope—a ray

of light had beamed forth, and enlightened minds thought to be in total darkness. Minds of no ordinary character, but those which embraced business, professions, and literature—minds, which at once grasped the earth, encompassed the seas, soared into the air, and mounted the skies. And it is none the less creditable to the colored people, that among those who have stood the most conspicuous and shone the brightest in the earliest period of our history, there are those of pure and unmixed African blood. A credit—but that which is creditable to the African, cannot disgrace any into whose veins his blood may chance to flow. The elevation of the colored man can only be completed by the elevation of the pure descendants of Africa; because to deny his equality, is to deny in a like proportion, the equality of all those mixed with the African organization; and to establish his inferiority, will be to degrade every person related to him by consanguinity; therefore, to establish the equality of the African with the European race, establishes the equality of every person intermediate between the two races. This establishes beyond contradiction, the general equality of men.

In the year 1773, though held in servitude, and without the advantages or privileges of the schools of the day, accomplishing herself by her own perseverance; Phillis Wheatley appeared in the arena, the brilliancy of whose genius, as a poetess, delighted Europe and astonished America, and by a special act of the British Parliament, 1773, her productions were published for the Crown. She was an admirer of President Washington, and addressed to him lines, which elicited from the Father of his country, a complimentary and courteous reply. In the absence of the poem addressed to General Washington, which was not written until after her work was published, we insert a stanza from one addressed (intended for the students) "To the University at Cambridge." We may further remark, that the poems were originally written, not with the most distant idea of publication, but simply for the amusement and during the leisure moments of the author.

> " Improve your privileges while they stay,
>   Ye pupils, and each hour redeem, that bears
>   Or good or bad report of you to heav'n.
>   Let sin, that baneful evil of the soul,
>   By you be shunn'd, nor once remit your guard ;
>   Suppress the deadly serpent in its egg.
>   Ye blooming plants of human race divine,
>   An *Ethiop* tells you 'tis your greatest foe ;
>   Its transient sweetness turns to endless pain,
>   And in immense perdition sinks the soul."

" CAMBRIDGE, FEBRRUARY 28, 1776.
" MISS PHILLIS :

" Your favor of the 26th of October, did not reach my hands till the middle of December. Time enough, you will say, to have given an answer ere this. Granted. But a variety of important occurrences, continually interposing to divert the mind and withdraw the attention, I hope will apologise for the delay, and plead my excuse for the seeming, but not real neglect. I thank you most sincerely for your

polite notice of me, in the elegant lines you enclosed ;
and however undeserving I may be of such encomium
and panegyric, the style and manner exhibit a striking proof of your poetic talents ; in honor of which,
and as a tribute justly due to you, I would have published the poem, had I not been apprehensive, that,
while I only meant to give the world this new instance of your genius, I might have incurred the
imputation of vanity. This, and nothing else, determined me not to give it place in the public prints.

"If you should ever come to Cambridge, or near
head-quarters, I shall be happy to see a person so
favored by the Muses, and to whom Nature has been
so liberal and beneficent in her dispensations.

"I am, with great respect, your obedient servant,
          "GEORGE WASHINGTON.
"Miss Phillis Wheatley."

The tenor, style, and manner of President Washington's letter to Miss Wheatley—the publication of
her works, together with an accompanying likeness
of the author, and her inscription and dedication of
the volume to the "Right Honorable the Countess of
Huntingdon," show, that she, though young, was a
person of no ordinary mind, no common attainments ;
but at the time, one of the brightest ornaments among
the American literati. She also was well versed in
Latin, in which language she composed several pieces.
Miss Wheatley died in 1780, at the age of 26 years,
being seven years of age when brought to this country
in 1761.

Doctor Peter, who married Miss Wheatley, 1775, was a man of business, tact, and talents—being first a grocer, and afterwards studied law, which he practised with great success, becoming quite wealthy by defending the cause of the oppressed before the different tribunals of the country. And who shone brighter in his day, than Benjamin Bannaker, of Baltimore county, Maryland, who by industry and force of character, became a distinguished mathematician and astronomer,—"for many years," says Davenport's Biographical Dictionary, " calculated and published the Maryland Ephemerides." He was a correspondent of the Honorable Thomas Jefferson, Secretary of State of the United States, taking the earliest opportunity of his acquaintanceship, to call his attention to the evils of American slavery, and doubtless his acquaintance with the apostle of American Democracy, had much to do with his reflections on that most pernicious evil in this country. Mr. Bannaker was also a naturalist, and wrote a treatise on locusts. He was invited by the Commission of United States Civil Engineers, to assist in the survey of the Ten Miles Square, for the District of Columbia. He assisted the Board, who, it is thought, could not have succeeded without him. His Almanac was preferred to that of Leadbeater, or any other calculator cotemporary with himself. He had no family, and resided in a house alone, but principally made his home with the Elliott family. He was upright, honorable, and virtuous; entertaining religious scruples similar to the Friends. He died in 1807, near Baltimore. Honorable John H. B. Latrobe, Esq., of Baltimore, is his biographer. In 1812, Captain Paul Cuffy was an extensive trader and mariner, sailing out of Boston, to the West Indies and Europe, by which enterprise, he amassed an immense fortune. He was known to the commercial world of his day, and, if not so wealthy, stood quite as fair, and as much respected, as Captain George Laws or Commodore Vanderbilt, the Cunards of America. Captain Cuffy went to Africa, where he died in a few years.

James Durham, originally of Philadelphia, in 1778, at the early age of twenty-one, was the most learned physician in New Orleans. He spoke English, French and Spanish, learnedly, and the great Dr. Rush said of him, " I conversed with him on medicine, and found him very learned. I thought I could give him information concerning the treatment of diseases; but I learned from him more than he could expect from me." And it must be admitted, he must have been learned in his profession, to have elicited such an encomium from Dr. Rush, who stood then at the head of his profession in the country.

We have designed nothing here, but merely to give an individual case of the various developments of talents and acquirements in the several departments of respectability, discarding generalization, and naming none but the Africo-American of unmixed extraction, who rose into note subsequent to the American Revolution. In the persons of note and distinction hereafter to be given, we shall not confine ourselves to any such narrow selections, but shall name persons, male and female, regardless of their extraction, so that they are colored persons, which is quite enough for our purpose. And our only excuse for the policy in the above course is, that we desire to disarm the villifiers of our race, who disparage us, giving themselves credit for whatever is commendable that may emanate from us, if there be the least opportunity of claiming it by " blood." We shall now proceed to review the attainments of colored men and women of the present day.

CHAPTER X.

PRACTICAL UTILITY OF COLORED PEOPLE OF THE PRESENT DAY AS MEMBERS OF SOCIETY — BUSINESS MEN AND MECHANICS.

IN calling attention to the practical utility of colored people of the present day, we shall not be general in our observations, but simply, direct attention to a few particular instances, in which colored persons have been responsibly engaged in extensive business, or occupying useful positions, thus contributing to the general welfare of community at large, filling their places in society as men and women.

It will studiously be borne in mind, that our sole object in giving these cases publicity, is to refute the objections urged against us, that we are not useful members of society. That we are consumers and non-producers—that we contribute nothing to the general progress of man. No people who have enjoyed no greater opportunity for improvement, could possibly have made greater progress in the same length of time than have done the colored people of the present day.

A people laboring under many disadvantages, may not be expected to present at once, especially before they have become entirely untrammeled, evidence of entire equality with more highly favored people.

When Mr. Jefferson, the great American Statesman and philosopher, was questioned by an English gentleman, on the subject of American greatness, and referred to their literature as an evidence of inferiority to the more highly favored and long-existing European nations ; Mr. Jefferson's reply was— " When the United States have existed as long as a nation, as Greece before she produced her Homer and Socrates ; Rome, before she produced her Virgil, Horace, and Cicero ; and England, before she produced her Pope, Dryden, and Bacon ;" then he might consider the comparison a just one. And all we shall ask, is not to wait so long as this, not to wait until we become a nation at all, so far as the United States are concerned, but only to unfetter our brethren, and give us, the freemen, an equal chance for emulation, and we will admit any comparison you may please to make in a quarter of a century after.

For a number of years, the late James Forten, of Philadelphia, was the proprietor of one of the principal sail manufactories, constantly employing a large number of men, black and white, supplying a large number of masters and owners of vessels, with full rigging for their crafts.

On the failure of an extensive house, T. & Co., in that city, during the pressure which followed a removal of the deposits of the United States Treasury in 1837, Mr. Forten lost by that firm, nine thousand dollars. Being himself in good circumstances at the time, hearing of the failure of old constant patrons, he called at the house; one of the proprietors, Mr. T., on his entering the warehouse door, came forward, taking him by the hand observed, "Ah! Mr. Forten, it is useless to call on us—we are gone—we can do nothing!" at which Mr. Forten remarked, "Sir, I hope you think better of me than to suppose me capable of calling on a friend to torture him in adversity! I came, sir, to express my regret at your misfortune, and if possible, to cheer you by words of encouragement. If your liabilities were all in my hands, you should never be under the necessity of closing business." Mr. Forten exchanged paper and signatures with some of the first business men in Philadelphia, and raised and educated a large and respectable family of sons and daughters, leaving an excellent widow.

Joseph Cassey, recently deceased, was the "archi-

tect of his own fortune," and by industry and
application to business, became a money broker in
the city of Philadelphia; who becoming indisposed
from a chronic affection, was obliged to retire from
business for many years previous to his death. Had
Mr. Cassey been favored with health, he doubtless
would have become a very wealthy man. His name
and paper was good in any house in the city, and
there was no banker of moderate capital, of more
benefit to the business community than was Joseph
Cassey. He also left a young and promising family
of five sons, one daughter, a most excellent widow,
and a fortune of seventy-five thousand dollars, clear
of all encumbrance.

Stephen Smith, of the firm of Smith and Whipper,
is a remarkable man in many respects, and decidedly
the most wealthy colored man in the United States.
Mr. Smith commenced business after he was thirty
years of age, without the advantages of a good
business education, but by application, qualified himself for the arduous duties of his vocation. For many
years, he has been known as the principal lumber
merchant in Columbia, Lancaster Co., Pa., and for
several years past associated with W. Whipper, a
gentleman of great force of character, talents, and
business qualifications, Mr. Smith residing in Philadelphia. Smith and Whipper, are very extensive
business men, and very valuable members of the
community, both of Lancaster and Philadelphia counties. By the judicious investment of their capital,
they keep in constant employment a large number of

persons; purchasing many rafts at a time, and many thousand bushels of coal. It is not only the laborer in "drawing boards," and the coal hauler and heaver, that are here benefitted by their capital, but the original owners of the lumber and coal purchased by them, and the large number of boatmen and raftsmen employed in bringing these commodities to market.

In the winter of 1849, these gentlemen had in store, several thousand bushels of coal, two million two hundred and fifty thousand feet of lumber; twenty-two of the finest merchantmen cars running on the railway from Philadelphia to Baltimore; nine thousand dollars' worth of stock in the Columbia Bridge; eighteen thousand dollars in stock in the Columbia Bank; and besides this, Mr. Smith was then the reputed owner of fifty-two good brick houses of various dimensions in the city of Philadelphia, besides several in the city of Lancaster, and the town of Columbia. Mr. Smith's paper, or the paper of the firm, is good for any amount wherever they are known; and we have known gentlemen to present the paper of some of the best men in the city, which was cashed by him at sight. The principal active business attended to by Mr. S. in person, is that of buying good negotiable and other paper, and speculating in real estate. The business of the firm is attended to by Mr. Whipper, who is a relative. Take Smith and Whipper from Lancaster and Philadelphia counties, and the business community will experience a hiatus in its connexion, that may not be easily filled.

Samuel T. Wilcox, of Cincinnati, Ohio, also stands conspicuously among the most respectable business men of the day. Being yet a young man, just scanning forty, he is one among the extraordinary men of the times. Born, like the most of colored men in this country, in obscurity, of poor parents, raised without the assistance of a father, and to a commonplace business, without the advantages of schools, by his own perseverance, he qualified himself to the extent that gave him an inclination to traffic, which he did for several years on the Mississippi and Ohio rivers, investing his gains in real estate, until he acquired a considerable property. For the purpose of extending his usefulness, and at the same time pursuing a vocation more in accordance with his own desires, a few years since, he embarked in the wholesale and retail Family Grocery business, and now has the best general assortment and most extensive business house of the kind, in the city of Cincinnati. The establishment is really beautiful, having the appearance more of an apothecary store, than a Grocery House. Mr. Wilcox has a Pickling and Preserving establishment besides, separate from his business house, owning a great deal of first class real estate. There is no man in the community in which he lives, that turns money to a greater advantage than Mr. Wilcox, and none by whom the community is more benefited for the amount of capital invested. He makes constant and heavy bills in eastern houses, and there are doubtless now many merchants in New York, Boston, and Baltimore cities, who have been

dealing with S. T. Wilcox, and never until the reading of this notice of him, knew that he was a colored
man. He has never yet been east after his goods,
but pursuing a policy which he has adopted, orders
them; but if deceived in an article, never deals with
the same house again. He always gets a good
article. The paper of Mr. Wilcox, is good for any
amount.

Henry Boyd, is also a man of great energy of
character, the proprietor of an extensive Bedstead
manufactory, with a large capital invested, giving
constant employment to eighteen or twenty-five men,
black and white. Some of the finest and handsomest
articles of the bedstead in the city, are at the
establishment of Mr. Boyd. He fills orders from all
parts of the West and South, his orders from the
South being very heavy. He is the patentee, or holds
the right of the Patent Bedsteads, and like Mr. Wilcox, there are hundreds who deal with Mr. Boyd at a
distance, who do not know that he is a colored man.
Mr. Boyd is a useful member of society, and Cincinnati would not, if she could, be without him. He fills
a place that every man is not capable of supplying,
of whatever quarter of the globe his forefathers may
have been denizens.

Messrs. Knight and Bell of the same place, Cincinnati, Ohio, are very successful and excellent mechanics.
In the spring of 1851, (one year ago) they put in
their " sealed proposal" for the plastering of the public buildings of the county of Hamilton—alms-house,
&c.—and got the contract, which required ten thou-

sand dollars' security. The work was finished in fine
artistic style, in which a large number of mechanics
and laborers were employed, while at the same time,
they were carrying on many other contracts of less
extent, in the city—the public buildings being some
four miles out. They are men of stern integrity, and
highly respected in the community.

David Jenkins of Columbus, Ohio, a good mechanic,
painter, glazier, and paper-hanger by trade, also received by contract, the painting, glazing, and paper-
ing of some of the public buildings of the State, in
autumn 1847. He is much respected in the capital city of his state, being extensively patronised,
having on contract, the great "Neill House," and
many of the largest gentlemen's residences in the
city and neighborhood, to keep in finish. Mr. Jenkins
is a very useful man and member of society.

John C. Bowers, for many years, has been the proprietor of a fashionable merchant tailor house, who
has associated with him in business, his brother
Thomas Bowers, said to be one of the best, if not the
very best, mercers in the city. His style of cutting
and fitting, is preferred by the first business men, and
other gentlemen of Philadelphia, in whom their patrons
principally consist.

Mr. Cordovell, for more than twenty-five years,
was the leading mercer and tailor, reporter and originator of fashions in the city of New Orleans, Louisiana. The reported fashions of Cordovell, are said to
have frequently become the leading fashions of Paris ;
and the writer was informed, by Mr. B., a leading

merchant tailor in a populous city, that many of the
eastern American reports were nothing more than a
copy, in some cases modified, of those of Cordovell.
Mr. Cordovell, has for the last four or five years, been
residing in France, living on a handsome fortune, the
fruits of his genius; and though "retired from business," it is said, that he still invents fashions for the
Parisian reporters, which yields him annually a large
income.

William H. Riley, of Philadelphia, has been for
years, one of the leading fashionable gentlemen's
boot-makers. Riley's style and cut of boots, taking
the preeminence in the estimation of a great many of
the most fashionable, and business men in the city.
Mr. Riley is much of a gentleman, and has acquired
considerable means.

James Prosser, Sen., of Philadelphia, has long been
the popular proprietor of a fashionable restaurant
in the city. The name of James Prosser, among the
merchants of Philadelphia, is inseparable with their
daily hours of recreation, and pleasure. Mr. Prosser,
is withal, a most gentlemanly man, and has the happy
faculty of treating his customers in such a manner,
that those who call once, will be sure to call at his place
again. His name and paper is good among the business
men of the city.

Henry Minton also is the proprietor of a fashionable restaurant and resort for business men and gentlemen of the city. The tables of Mr. Henry
Minton are continually laden with the most choice
offerings to epicures, and the saloon during certain

hours of the day, presents the appearance of a bee hive, such is the stir, din, and buz, among the throng of Chesnut street gentlemen, who flock in there to pay tribute at the shrine of bountifulness. Mr. Minton has acquired a notoriety, even in that proud city, which makes his house one of the most popular resorts.

Mr. Hill, of Chillicothe, Ohio, was for years, the leading tanner and currier in that section of country, buying up the hides of the surrounding country, and giving employment to large numbers of men. Mr. Hill kept in constant employment, a white clerk, who once a year took down, as was then the custom, one or more flatboats loaded with leather and other domestic produce, by which he realised large profits, accumulating a great deal of wealth. By endorsement, failure, and other mistransactions, Mr. Hill became reduced in circumstances, and died in Pittsburgh, Pennsylvania, in 1845. He gave his children a liberal business education.

Benjamin Richards, sen., of Pittsburgh, Pennsylvania, forty years ago, was one of the leading business men of the place. Being a butcher by trade, he carried on the business extensively, employing a white clerk, and held a heavy contract with the United States, supplying the various military posts with provisions. Mr. Richards possessed a large property in real estate, and was at one time reputed very wealthy, he and the late general O'H. being considered the most wealthy individuals of the place,—Mr. Richards taking the precedence; the estate of general O'H. now being estimated at seven millions of dollars. Mr.

Richards has been known, to buy up a drove of cattle at one time. By mismanagement, he lost his estate, upon which many gentlemen are now living at ease in the city.

William H. Topp, of Albany, N. Y., has for several years been one of the leading merchant tailors of the city. Starting in the world without aid, he educated and qualified himself for business ; and now has orders from all parts of the state, the city of New York not excepted, for " Topp's style of clothing." Mr. Topp stands high in his community as a business man, and a useful and upright member of society. His paper or endorsement is good at any time.

Henry Scott & Co., of New York city, have for many years been engaged extensively in the pickling business, keeping constantly in warehouse, a very heavy stock of articles in their line.   He, like the most of others, had no assistance at the commencement, but by manly determination and perseverance, raised himself to what he is.   His business is principally confined to supplying vessels with articles and provisions in his line of business, which in this great metropolis is very great.   There have doubtless been many a purser, who cashed and filed in his office the bill of Henry Scott, without ever dreaming of his being a colored man.   Mr. Scott is extensively known in the great City, and respected as an upright, prompt, energetic business man, and highly esteemed by all who know him.

Mr. Hutson, for years, kept in New York, an intelligence office. At his demise, he was succeeded by Philip

A. Bell, who continues to keep one of the leading offices in the city. Mr. Bell is an excellent business man, talented, prompt, shrewd, and full of tact. And what seems to be a trait of character, only to be found associated with talent, Mr. Bell is highly sensitive, and very eccentric. A warm, good hearted man, he has not only enlisted the friendship of all his patrons, but also endeared himself to the multitude of persons who continually throng his office seeking situations. One of his usual expressions to the young women and men in addressing himself to them is, "My child"—this is kind, and philanthropic, and has a tendency to make himself liked. His business is very extensive, being sought from all parts of the city, by the first people of the community. It is said to be not unusual, for the peasantry of Liverpool, to speak of Mr. Bell, as a benefactor of the emigrant domestics. Mr. Bell is extensively known in the business community—none more so—and highly esteemed as a valuable citizen.

Thomas Downing, for thirty years, in the city of New York, has been proprietor of one of the leading restaurants. His establishment situated in the midst of the Wall street bankers, the business has always been of a leading and profitable character. Mr. Downing has commanded great influence, and much means, and it is said of him that he has made "three fortunes." Benevolent, kind, and liberal minded, his head was always willing, his heart ready, and his hands open to "give." Mr. Downing is still very popular, doing a most excellent business, and highly respected throughout New York. Indeed, you scarcely hear any other establishment of the kind spoken of than Downing's.

Henry M. Collins, of the City of Pittsburg, stands among the men of note ; and we could not complete this list of usefulness, without the name of Mr. Collins. Raised a poor boy, thrown upon the uncertainties of chance, without example or precept, save such as the public at large presents ; Mr. Collins quit his former vocation of a riverman, and without means, except one hundred and fifty dollars, and no assistance from any quarter, commenced speculating in real estate.   And though only rising forty, has done more to improve the Sixth Ward of Pittsburg, than any other individual, save one, Captain W., who built on Company capital.   Mr. Collins was the first person who commenced erecting an improved style of buildings; indeed, there was little else than old trees in that quarter of the city when Mr. Collins began.   He continued to build, and dispose of handsome dwellings, until a different class of citizens entirely, was attracted to that quarter of the town, among them, one of the oldest and most respectable and wealthy citizens, an ex-Alderman.   After this, the wealthy citizens turned their attention to the District ; and now, it is one of the most fashionable quarters of the City, and bids fair to become, the preferred part for family residences.   Mr. Collins' advice and counsel was solicited by some of the first lawyers, and land speculators, in matters of real estate.   He has left, or contemplates leaving Pittsburg, in April, for California, where he intends entering extensively into land speculation, and doubtless, with the superior advantages of this place, if his success is but half what it was in the former, but a few years will find him counted among the wealthy. Mr. Collins is a highly valuable man in any community in which he may live, and he leaves Pittsburg much to the regret of the leading citizens. Without capital, he had established such a reputation, that his name and paper were good in some of the first Banking houses.

Owen A. Barrett of Pittsburg, Pa., is the original proprietor of "B. A. Fahnestock's Celebrated Vermifuge." Mr. Fahnestock raised Mr. Barrett from childhood, instructing him in all the science of practical pharmacy, continuing him in his employment after manhood, when Mr. Barrett discovered the "sovereign remedy" for *lumbricalii*, and as an act of gratitude to his benefactor, he communicated it to him, but not until he had fully tested its efficacy. The proprietor of the house, finding the remedy good, secured his patent, or copy right, or whatever is secured, and never in the history of remedies in the United States, has any equaled, at least in sale, this of "B. A. Fahnestock's Vermifuge." Mr. Fahnestock, like a gentleman and Christian, has kept Mr. Barrett in his extensive House, compounding this and other medicines, for sixteen or eighteen years.

In 1840 it was estimated, that of this article alone, the concern had realized eighty-five thousand dollars. Doubtless, this is true, and certainly proves Mr. Barrett to be of benefit, not only in his community, but like many others we have mentioned, to the country and the world.

Lewis Hayden, of Boston, is well deserving a place among the examples of character here given. But eight years ago, having emerged from bondage, he raised by his efforts, as an act of gratitude and duty, six hundred and fifty dollars, the amount demanded by mutual agreement, by the authorities in Kentucky, as a ransom for Calvin Fairbanks, then in the State Prison, at Frankfort, accused for assisting him in effecting his escape. In 1848, he went to Boston, and having made acquaintance, and gained confidence with several business men, Mr. Hayden opened a fashionable Clothing House in Cambridge street, where he has within the last year, enlarged his establishment, being patronized by some of the most respectable citizens of that wealthy Metropolis. Mr. Hayden has made considerable progress, considering his disadvantages, in his educational improvements. He has great energy of character, and extensive information. Lewis Hayden by perseverance, may yet become a very wealthy man. He is generally esteemed by the Boston people—all seeming to know him.

George T. Downing, a gentleman of education and fine business attainments, is proprietor of one of the principal Public houses and places of resort, at Newport, Rhode Island, during the watering Season. This fashionable establishment is spoken of as among the best conducted places in the country—the Proprietor among the most gentlemanly.

Edward V. Clark, is among the most deserving and

active business men in New York, and but a few years are required, to place Mr. Clark in point of business importance, among the first men in the city. His stock consists of Jewelry and Silver Wares, and consequently, are always valuable, requiring a heavy capital to keep up business. His name and paper, has a respectable credit, even among the urbane denizens of Wall street.

John Julius and Lady, were for several years, the Proprietors of Concert Hall, a *Caffé*, then the most fashionable resort for ladies and gentlemen in Pittsburg. Mr. and Mrs. Julius, held Assemblies and Balls, attended by the first people of the city—being himself a fine violinist and dancing master, he superintended the music and dancing. When General William Henry Harrison in 1840, then the President elect of the United States, visited that city, his levee to and reception of the Ladies were held at Concert Hall, under the superintendence of Monsieur John and Madame Edna Julius, the colored host and hostess. No House was ever better conducted than under their fostering care, and excellent management, and the citizens all much regretted their retirement from the establishment.

In Penyan, Western New York, Messrs. William Platt and Joseph C. Cassey, are said to be the leading Lumber Merchants of the place. Situated in the midst of a great improving country, their business extends, and increases in importance every year. The latter gentleman was raised to the business by Smith and Whipper, the great Lumber Merchants of

Columbia, Pa., where he was principal Book-Keeper for several years. Mr. Cassey has the credit of being one of the best Accountants, and Business Men in the United States of his age. Doubtless, a few years' perseverance, and strict application to business, will find them ranked among the most influential men of their neighborhood.

Anthony Weston, of Charleston, South Carolina, has acquired an independent fortune, by his mechanical ingenuity, and skillful workmanship. About the year 1831, William Thomas Catto, mentioned in another place, commenced an improvement on a Thrashing Machine, when on taking sick, Mr. Weston improved on it, to the extent of thrashing a thousand bushels a day. This Thrashing Mill, was commenced by a Yankee, by the name of Emmons, who failing to succeed, Mr. Catto, then a Millwright—since a Minister—improved it to the extent of thrashing five hundred bushels a day; when Mr. Weston, took it in hand, and brought it to the perfection stated, for the use of Col. Benjamin Franklin Hunt, a distinguished lawyer of Charleston, upon whose plantation, the machine was built, and to whom it belonged. Anthony Weston, is the greatest Millwright in the South, being extensively employed far and near, and by Southern people, thought the best in the United States.

Dereef and Howard, are very extensive Wood-Factors, keeping a large number of men employed, a regular Clerk and Book-Keeper, supplying the citizens, steamers, vessels, and factories of Charleston with fuel. In this business a very heavy capital is invested:

besides which, they are the owners and proprietors of several vessels trading on the coast. They are men of great business habits, and command a great deal of respect and influence in the city of Charleston.

There is nothing more common in the city of New Orleans, than Colored Clerks, Salesmen and Business men. In many stores on Chartier, Camp and other business streets, there may always be seen colored men and women, as salesmen, and saleswomen, behind the counter. Several of the largest Cotton-Press houses, have colored Clerks in them ; and on the arrival of steamers at the Levees, among the first to board them, and take down the Manifestos to make their transfers, are colored Clerks. In 1839—40, one of the most respectable Brokers and Bankers of the City, was a black gentleman.

Mr. William Goodrich of York, Pennsylvania, has considerable interest in the branch of the Baltimore Railroad, from Lancaster. In 1849, he had a warehouse in York, and owned ten first-rate merchandise cars on the Road, doing a fine business. His son, Glenalvon G. Goodrich, a young man of good education, is a good artist, and proprietor of a Daguerreotype Gallery.

Certainly, there need be no farther proofs required, at least in this department, to show the claims and practical utility of colored people as citizen members of society. We have shown, that in proportion to their numbers, they vie and compare favorably in point of means and possessions, with the class of citizens who from chance of superior advantages, have studiously contrived to oppress and deprive them of equal rights and privileges, in common with them selves.

———◦•◦———

CHAPTER XI.

LITERARY AND PROFESSIONAL COLORED MEN AND WOMEN.

DR. JAMES MCCUNE SMITH, a graduate of the Scientific and Medical Schools of the University of Glasgow, has for the last fifteen years, been a successful practitioner of medicine and surgery in the city of New York. Dr. Smith is a man of no ordinary talents, and stands high as a scholar and gentleman in the city, amidst the *literati* of a hundred seats of learning.

In 1843, when the character of the colored race was assailed to disparagement, by the representative of a combination of maligners, such was the influence of the Doctor, that the citizens at once agreed to give their presence to a fair public discussion of the subject—the Comparative Anatomy and Physiology of the races. This discussion was kept up for several evenings, attended by large and fashionable assemblages of ladies and gentlemen, until it closed. Doctor Smith, in the estimation of the audience, easily

PROFESSIONAL COLORED MEN.   **111**

triumphed over his antagonist, who had made this a studied subject. The Doctor is the author of several valuable productions, and in 1846, a very valuable scientific paper, issued from the press in pamphlet form, on the "Influence of Climate on Longevity, with special reference to Life Insurance." This paper, we may surmise, was produced in refutation of the attempt at a physiological disquisition on the part of Hon. John C. Calhoun, United States Senator, on the colored race, which met with considerable favor from some quarters, until the appearance of Dr. Smith's pamphlet—since when, we have heard nothing about Calhoun's learned argument. It may be well to re- mark, that Senator Calhoun read medicine before he read law, and it would have been well for him if he had left medical subjects remain where *he left* them, for law. We extract a simple note of explanation without the main argument, to show with what ease the Doctor refutes an absurd argument : " The reason why the proportion of mortality is not a measure of longevity, is the following :—The proportion of mor- tality is a statement of how many persons die in a population ; this, of course, does not state the age at which those persons die. If 1 in 45 die in Sweden, and 1 in 22 in Grenada, the ages of the dead might be alike in both countries ; here the greater mor- tality might actually accompany the greater longe- vity."—Note to page 6.

About three months since, at a public meeting of scientific gentlemen, for the formation of a "Statistic Institute," Doctor Smith was nominated as one of five gentlemen, to draught a constitution. This, of course, anticipated his membership to the Institution. He, for a number of years, has held the office of Physician to the Colored Orphan Asylum, an excellent institution, at which he is the only colored officer. The Doctor is very learned.

Rev. Samuel Ringgold Ward was, for several years, pastor of a white congregation, in Courtlandville, N. Y., of the Congregational persuasion, and editor of an excellent newspaper, devoted to the religious elevation of that denomination. Mr. Ward is a man of great talents—his fame is widespread as an orator and man of learning, and needs no encomium from us. His name stood on nomination for two or three years, as Liberty-party candidate for Vice President of the United States. Mr. Ward has embraced the legal profession, and intends to practise law. Governor Seward said of him, that he " never heard true eloquence until he heard Samuel R. Ward speak." Mr. Ward has recently left the United States, for Canada West, and is destined to be a great statesman.

Rev. Henry Highland Garnett, was also the pastor of a white congregation, in Troy, N. Y. Mr. Garnett is a graduate of Oneida Institute, a speaker of great pathetic eloquence, and has written several valuable pamphlets. In 1844, Mr. Garnett appeared before the Judiciary Committee of the Legislature at the capital, in behalf of the rights of the colored citizens of the State, and in a speech of matchless eloquence, he held them for four hours spell-bound.

He has also been co-editor of a newspaper, which

was conducted with ability. As a token of respect, the "Young Men's Literary Society of Troy," elected him a life-member—and he was frequently solicited to deliver lectures before different lyceums. Mr. Garnett left the United States in the summer of 1849, and now resides in England, where he is highly esteemed.

Rev. James William Charles Pennington, D. D., a clergyman of New York city, was born in Maryland, —left when young—came to Brooklyn—educated himself—studied divinity—went to Hartford, Conn.;—took charge of a Presbyterian congregation of colored people—went to England—returned—went to the West Indies—returned—was called to the Shiloh Presbyterian Colored Congregation—was sent a Delegate to the Peace Congress at Paris, in 1849, preached there, and attended the National Levee at the mansion of the For-eign Secretary of State, Minister De Tocqueville ; and had the degree of *Doctor of Divinity* conferred on him by the ancient time-honored University of Hiedleburg, in Germany.

Dr. Pennington is very learned in theology, has fine literary attainments, and has written several useful pamphlets, and contributed to science, by the delivery of lectures before several scientific institutions in Europe.

He has, by invitation, delivered lectures before the "Glasgow Young Men's Christian Association ;" and "St. George's Biblical, Literary, and Scientific Institute," London. In one of the discourses, the following extract will give an idea of the style and character of the speaker :—"One of the chief attributes of

the mind is a desire for freedom ; but it has been the
great aim of slavery to extinguish that desire."

"To extinguish this attribute would be to extinguish
mind itself. Every faculty which the master puts
forth to subdue the slave, is met by a corresponding
one in the latter." * * * "Christianity is the
highest and most perfect form of civilization. It contains the only great standard of the only true and
perfect standard of civilization. When tried by this
standard, we are compelled to confess, that we have
not on earth, one strictly civilized nation ; for so long
as the sword is part of a nation's household furniture,
it cannot be called strictly civilized ; and yet there is
not a nation, great or small, black or white, that has
laid aside the sword."—pp. 7–14. The Doctor has
been editor of a newspaper, which was ably conducted.
He belongs to the Third Presbytery of New York, and
stands very high as a minister of the Gospel, and gentleman.

Rev. John Francis Cook, a learned clergyman of
Washington City, has taught an academy in the District of Columbia for years, under the subscribed sanc-
tion and patronage of many of the members of Congress, the Mayor of Washington, and some of the first
men of the nation, for the education of colored youth
of both sexes. Mr. Cook has done a great deal of
good at the Capitol; is highly esteemed, and has set
as Moderator of a body of Presbyterian Clergymen,
assembled at Richmond, Va., all white, except himself.

Charles L. Reason, Esq., a learned gentleman, for
many years teacher in one of the Public Schools in

New York, in 1849, was elected by the trustees of that institution, Professor of Mathematics and Belles Lettres in Centre College, at McGrawville, in the State of New York. After a short connection with the College, Professor Reason, for some cause, retired from the Institution, much to the regret of the students, who, though a young man, loved him as an elder brother—and contrary to the desire of his fellow-professors.

Mr. Reason is decidedly a man of letters, a high-souled gentleman, a most useful citizen in any community—much respected and beloved by all who know him, and most scrupulously modest—a brilliant trait in the character of a teacher. We learn that Professor Reason, is about to be called to take charge of the High School for the education of colored youth of both sexes, now in course of completion in Philadelphia. The people of New York will regret to part with Professor Reason.

Charles Lenox Remond, Esq., of Salem, Massachusetts, is among the most talented men of the country. Mr. Remond is a native of the town he resides in, and at an early age, evinced more than ordinary talents. At the age of twenty-one, at which time (1832) the cause of the colored people had just begun to attract public attention, he began to take an interest in public affairs, and was present for the first time, at the great convention of colored men, of that year, at which the distinguished colonization gentlemen named in another part of this work, among them, Rev. R. R. Gurley, and Elliot Cresson, Esqs., were

present. At this convention, we think, Mr. Remond
made his virgin speech. From that time forth he became
known as an orator, and now stands second to no
living man as a declaimer. This is his great forte, and
to hear him speak, sends a thrill through the whole
system, and a tremor through the brain.

In 1835, he went to England, making a tour of the
United Kingdom, where he remained for two years,
lecturing with great success ; and if we mistake not
was presented the hospitality of one of the towns of
Scotland, at which he received a token of respect, in
a code of resolutions adopted expressive of the sentiments of the people, signed by the town officers, in-
scribed to " Charles Lenox Remond, Esq.," a form of
address never given in the United Kingdom, only
where the person is held in the highest esteem for
their attainments ; the " Mr." always being used
instead.

To C. L. Remond, are the people of Massachusetts
indebted for the abolition of the odious distinction of
caste, on account of condition. For up to this period,
neither common white, nor genteel colored persons,
could ride in first class cars ; since which time, all who
are able and willing to pay, go in them. In fact, there
is but one class of cars, (except the emigrant cars which
are necessary for the safety and comfort of other pas-
sengers) in Massachusetts.

Mr. Remond, appeared at one time before the legislature of Massachusetts, in behalf of the rights of the
people above named, where with peals of startling
eloquence, he moved that great body of intelligent

New Englanders, to a respectful consideration of his subject; which eventually resulted as stated. The distinguished Judge Kelley, of Philadelphia, an accomplished scholar and orator, in 1849, in reply to an expression that Mr. Remond spoke like himself, observed, that it was the greatest compliment he ever had paid to his talents. "Proud indeed should I feel," said the learned Jurist, "were I such an orator as Mr. Remond." Charles Lenox Remond is the soul of an honorable gentleman.

Robert Morris, Jr., Esq., attorney and counsellor at law, is a member of the Essex county bar in Boston. Mr. Morris has also had the commission of magistracy conferred upon him, by his excellency George N. Briggs, recent governor of the commonwealth of Massachusetts, a high honor and compliment to an Attorney; the commission usually being conferred on none but the oldest or most meritorious among the members of the bar. He also keeps the books of one of the wealthy rail road companies, a business almost entirely confined to lawyers in that city. Mr. Morris is a talented gentleman, and stands very high at the Boston bar. He sometimes holds the magistrate's court in Chelsea, where his family resides, and is very highly esteemed by the whole community of both cities, and has a fine practice.

Macon B. Allen, Esq., attorney and counsellor at law, is also a member of the Essex bar. He is spoken of as a gentleman of fine education.

Robert Douglass, Jr., for many years, has kept a study and gallery of painting and daguerreotype in the city of Philadelphia. Mr. Douglass is an excellent artist—being a fine portrait and landscape painter, which art he practised before the discovery of daguerreotype. He is also a good lithographer, a gentleman of fine educational attainments, very clever talents, and highly esteemed in that city. Mr. Douglass has been twice to the West Indies and Europe.

J. Presley Ball is the principal daguerreotypist of Cincinnati, Ohio. Mr. Ball commenced the practice of his art about seven years ago, being then quite young, and inexperienced, as all young beginners are, laboring under many difficulties. He nevertheless, persevered, until he made a business, and established confidence in his skill ; and now he does more business than any other artist in the profession in that city. His gallery, which is very large, finely skylighted, and handsomely furnished, is literally crowded from morning until evening with ladies, gentlemen, and children. He made some valuable improvements in the art, all for his own convenience. There is none more of a gentleman than J. Presley Ball. He has a brother, Mr. Thomas Ball, and a white gentleman to assist him. Few go to Cincinnati, without paying the daguerrean gallery of Mr. Ball, a visit.

The great organ of the "Liberty Party" in the United States, is now conducted by one who requires not a notice from such an obscure source—we mean Frederick Douglass, of Rochester, N. Y. His history is well known—it was written by more faithful hands than ours—it was written by himself. It stands enrolled on the reminiscences of Germany, and

France, and in full length oil, in the academy of arts, and in bust of bronze or marble, in the museum of London. Mr. Douglass is also the sole owner of the printing establishment from which the paper is issued, and was promoted to this responsible position, by the power of his talents. He is a masterly letter writer, ably edits his paper, and as a speaker, and orator, let the scenes of a New York tabernacle, within two years, answer instead. Mr. Douglass is highly respected as a citizen and gentleman in Rochester.

In Syracuse, N. Y., resides George Boyer Vashon, Esq., A. M., a graduate of Oberlin Collegiate Institute, Attorney at Law, Member of the Syracuse Bar. Mr. Vashon, is a ripe scholar, an accomplished Essayist, and a chaste classic Poet; his style running very much in the strain of Byron's best efforts. He probably takes Byron as his model, and Childe Harold, as a sample, as in his youthful days, he was a fond admirer of GEORGE GORDON NOEL BYRON, always calling his whole name, when he named him. His Preceptor in Law, was the Honorable Walter, Judge Forward, late Controller, subsequently, Secretary of the Treasury of the United States, and recently *Charge de Affaires* to Denmark, now President of the Bench of the District Court of the Western District of Pennsylvania.

Mr. Vashon was admitted to the Bar of the city of New York, in the fall of 1847, to practise in all the Courts of the State. He immediately subsequently, sailed to the West Indies, from whence he returned

in the fall of 1850.   He has contributed considerably
to a number of the respectable journals of the country.

Mrs. Ann Maria Johnson, of the School of Mrs.
Tillman and Mrs. Johnson, Teachers in French Wors-
ted Needle Work, at the Exhibition of the Mechanics'
Institute in Chicago, Ill., 1846, took the First Prize,
and got her Diploma, for the best embroidery in cloth.
This was very flattering to those ladies, especially the
Diplomast, considering the great odds they had to
contend with.   The ladies were very successful teachers—their classes were always large.

In Williamsburg there is T. Joiner White, M. D.;
in Brooklyn Peter Ray, M. D.; and in the city of
New York, also, John Degrass, M. D., all young Physicians, who have time and experience yet before them,
and promise fair to be good and useful members of
society.

Miss Eliza Greenfield the BLACK SWAN, is among
the most extraordinary persons of the present century.
Being raised in obscurity, inured to callings far beneath her propensity, and unsuited to her taste, she
had a desire to cultivate her talents, but no one to encourage her.   Whenever she made the effort, she was
discouraged—perhaps ridiculed; and thus discouraged,
she would shrink again from her anxious task.   She
knew she could sing, and knew she could sing unlike
any body else; knew she sung better than any whom
she had heard of the popular singers, but could not
tell why others could not think with, and appreciate
her.   In this way it seems, she was thrown about for
three years, never meeting with a person who could

fully appreciate her talents ; and we have it from her own lips, that not until after the arrival of Jenny Lind and Parodi in the country, was she aware of the high character of her own talents.   She knew she possessed them, because they were inherent, inseparable with her being.   She attended the Concerts of Mad'll. Jenny Lind, and Operas of Parodi, and at once saw the " secret of their success"—they possessed talents, that no other popular singers mastered.

She went home ; her heart fluttered ; she stole an opportunity when no one listened, to mock or gossip ; let out her voice, when *ecce !* she found her strains *four* notes *above* Sweden's favored Nightingale; she descended, when lo ! she found her tones *three* notes *below !* she thanked God with a " still small voice ;" and now, she ranks second in point of voice, to no vocalist in the world.   Miss Greenfield, if she only be judicious and careful, may become yet, in point of popularity, what Miss Lind was.   The Black Swan, is singing to fine fashionable houses, and bids fair to stand unrivalled in the world of Song.

Patrick Henry Reason, a gentleman of ability and fine artist, stands high as an Engraver in the city of New York.   Mr. Reason has been in business for years, in that city, and has sent out to the world, many beautiful specimens of his skillful hand.   He was the first artist, we believe in the United States, who produced a plate of that beautiful touching little picture, the Kneeling Slave ; the first picture of which represented a handsome, innocent little girl upon her knees, with hands outstretched, leaving the manacles dangling before her, anxiously looking and wishfully asking, "*Am I not a sister?*" It was beautiful—sorrowfully beautiful. He has we understand, frequently done Government engraving. Mr. P: H. is a brother of Professor Charles L. Reason.

David Jones Peck, M. D., a graduate of Rush Medical College, a talented young gentleman, practised Medicine for two years in Philadelphia. He left there in 1850.

William H. Allen, Esq., A. B., successor to Professor C. L. Reason, is Professor of Languages in Centre College, at McGrawville, N. Y. Professor Allen, is a gentleman of fine education, a graduate of Oneida Institute, and educated himself entirely by his own industry, having the aid of but fifty dollars during the whole period. The Professor is a talented Lecturer on Ancient History, and much of a gentleman.

Martin H. Freeman, A. B., a young gentleman, graduate of Rutland College, in Vermont, is " Junior Professor," in Allegheny Institute, Allegheny county, Pa. The Professor is a gentleman of talents, and doing much good in his position.

Rev. Molliston Madison Clark, a gentleman of great talents, a noble speaker, educated at. Jefferson College, Pa., sailed to Europe in 1846, and was a member of the Evangelical Alliance. Mr. Clark kept a regular Journal of his travels through the United Kingdom of England, Scotland and Ireland. As well as a Greek and Latin, he is also a French and Spanish Linguist. He has all the eccentricity of Rowland Hill, manifested only in a very different manner.

William C. Nell, of Rochester, N. Y., formerly of Boston, has long been known as a gentleman of chaste and lofty sentiments, and a pure philanthropist. Mr. Nell, in company with Mr. Frederick Douglass, was present by invitation, and took his seat at table, at the celebration of Franklin's Birth Day, by the Typographical and Editorial corps of Rochester. In 1850, being again residing in Boston, he was nominated and ran for the Legislature of Massachusetts, by the Free Soil party of Essex county. Mr. Nell stood even with his party vote in the District.

He recently issued from the Boston press a Pamphlet, on the colored men who served in the wars of the United States of 1776, and 1812. This pamphlet is very useful as a book of reference on this subject, and Mr. Nell, of course does not aim at a full historical view. The circumstances under which it was got out, justify this belief. He was collecting materials in the winter of 1850–'51, when he was taken down to his bed with a severe attack of disease of one of his lungs, with which he lingered, unable to leave his room for weeks. In the Spring, recovering somewhat his health, so as to go out—during this time, he had the little pamphlet published, as a means of pecuniary aid, promising another part to be forthcoming some subsequent period, which the writer hopes may soon be issued. Mr. Nell, is an excellent man, and deserves the patronage of the public.

Joseph G. Anderson, successor to Captain Frank Johnson, of Philadelphia, is now one of the most distinguished musicians in the country. Mr. Anderson is an artist professionally and practically, mastering various instruments, a composer of music, and a gentleman of fine accomplishments in other respects. His musical fame will grow with his age, which one day must place him in the front ranks of his profession, among the masters in the world.

William Jackson, is among the leading musicians of New York city, and ranks among the most skillful violinists of America. This gentleman is a master of his favorite instrument, executing with ease the most difficult and critical composition. He is generally preferred in social and private parties, among the first families of the city, where the amateur and gentleman is more regarded than the mere services of the musician. Mr. Jackson is a teacher of music, and only requires a more favorable opportunity to vie with Ole Bull or Paganini.

Rev. Daniel A. Payne, commenced his literary career in Charleston, South Carolina, where he taught school for some time. In 1833 or 1834, he came North, placing himself in the Lutheran Theological Seminary, at Gettysburg, under the tutorage of the learned and distinguished Dr. Schmucker, where he finished his education as a Lutheran clergyman. To extend his usefulness, he joined the African Methodist Connexion, and for several years resided in Baltimore, where he taught an Academy for colored youth and maidens, gaining the respect and esteem of all who had the fortune to become acquainted with him. He is now engaged travelling and collecting information, for the publication of a history of one of the

colored Methodist denominations in the United States.
Mr. Payne is a pure and chaste poet, having published a small volume of his productions in 1850,
under the title of "Pleasures and other Miscella-
neous Poems, by Daniel A. Payne," issued from
the press of Sherwood and Company, Baltimore,
Maryland.

Rev. William T. Catto, a clergyman of fine talents,
finished his education in the Theological Seminary in
Charleston, South Carolina. He was ordained by
the Presbytery of Charleston, and in 1848, under the
best recommendations for piety, acquirements, and
all the qualifications necessary to his high mission as
a clergyman, was sent out as a missionary to preach
the Gospel to all who needed it ; but to make himself
more useful, he joined the African Methodist Episcopal Church Connexion, and is now a useful and successful preacher in Philadelphia.

The musical profession of Philadelphia has long
had a valuable votary in the person of William
Appo, an accomplished pianist. Mr. Appo has been
a teacher of the piano forte, for more than twenty
years, alternately in the cities of New York and Philadelphia, and sometimes in Baltimore. His profession extends amongst the citizens generally, from
the more moderate in circumstances, to the ladies and
daughters of the most wealthy gentlemen in community. This gentleman is a fine scholar, and as well
as music, teaches the French language successfully.
His young daughter, Helen, a miss of fourteen
years of age, inherits the musical talents of her

father, and is now organist in the central Presbyterian Church. The name of William Appo, is generally known as a popular teacher of music, but few who are not personally acquainted with him, know that he is a colored gentleman.

Augustus Washington, an artist of fine taste and perception, is numbered among the most successful Daguerreotypists in Hartford, Connecticut. His establishment is said to be visited daily by large numbers of the citizens of all classes; and this gallery is perhaps, the only one in the country, that keeps a female attendant, and dressing-room for ladies. He recommends, in his cards, black dresses to be worn for sitting; and those who go unsuitably dressed, are supplied with drapery, and properly enrobed.

John Newton Templeton, A. M., for fifteen years an upright, active, and very useful citizen of Pittsburg, Pennsylvania, was a graduate of Athens College, in the State of Ohio. Mr. Templeton, after an active life of more than twenty years, principally spent in school teaching, died in Pittsburg, in July, 1851, leaving an amiable widow and infant son.

Thomas Paul, A. B., of Boston, a gentleman of fine talents and amiable disposition, whose life has been mainly devoted to teaching, is a graduate of Bowdoin College, in Maine. Mr. Paul is now the recipient of a salary of fifteen hundred dollars a year as teacher of a school in Boston.

Rev. Benjamin Franklin Templeton, pastor of St. Mary street Church, Philadelphia, was educated at Hanover College, near Madison, Indiana. In 1838,

Mr. Templeton was ordained a minister of the Ripley
Presbytery, in Ohio; subsequently, in 1841, established a church, the Sixth Presbyterian, in Pittsburg,
Pennsylvania, from which place he was called, in
1844, to take charge of his present pastorate. Mr.
Templeton is a beautiful speaker, and an amiable
gentleman.*

* During the last twenty years, there have been, at different periods,
published among the colored people of the United States, twenty odd
newspapers, some of which were conducted with ability. Among
them, the "Colored American," in New York city; Samuel E. Cornish, Philip A. Bell, and Charles B. Ray, at different times, Editors.
"The Demosthenian Shield," issued from a Literary Society of young
colored men, in the city of Philadelphia. "The Struggler," by
Philip A. Bell, New York, out of which the Colored American took
its origin. The "National Reformer," an able monthly periodical, in
pamphlet form, in Philadelphia; William Whipper, Editor. "The
Northern Star," a Temperance monthly newspaper, published in Al-
bany, N. Y.; Stephen Myers, Editor, still in existence—changed to
————————. "The Mystery," of Pittsburg, Pa.; Martin Robison Delany, Editor—succeeded by a committee of colored gentlemen as Editors. The "Palladium of Liberty," issued in Columbus,
O., by a committee of colored gentlemen; David Jenkins, Editor.
"The Disfranchised American," by a committee of colored gentlemen,
Cincinnati, O.; A. M. Sumner, Editor—succeeded by the "Colored
Citizen;" Rev. Thomas Woodson, and William Henry Yancey, Edi-
tors. The "National Watchman," Troy, N. Y.; William H. Allen
and Henry Highland Garnett, Editors. Another issued in New York
city, the name of which, we cannot now remember; James William
Charles Pennington, D. D., and James McCuen Smith, M. D., Edi-
tors: the issue being alternately at Hartford, the then residence of
Dr. Pennington—and New York city, the residence of Dr. Smith.
The "Excelsior," an ephemeral issue, which appeared but once, in
Detroit, Mich.; William H. Day, Editor.
    The "Christian Herald," the organ of the A. M. Episcopal Church,
published under the auspices of the General Conference of that body;

John B. Russworm, a gentleman of splendid talents, graduated at Bowdoin College, many years ago. Mr. Russworm was a class-mate of Honorable John P.

Augustus Richardson Green, Editor, and General Book Steward. This gentleman has, also, written and published several small volumes of a religious character; a pamphlet on the Episcopacy and Infant Baptism, and the Lives of Reverends Fayette Davis and David Canyou. The "Elevator," of Philadelphia; James McCrummill, Editor. The "Ram's Horn," New York city; Thomas Vanrensallear, Editor. There is now a little paper, the name of which we cannot recollect, issued at Newark, N. J., merely a local paper, very meager in appearance. "The Farmer and Northern Star," in Courtland, N. Y., afterwards changed to the "Impartial Citizen," and published in Boston; Samuel Ringgold Ward, Editor. "The North Star," published in Rochester, N. Y.; Frederick Douglass, and Martin Robison Delany, Editors—subsequently changed to the "Frederick Douglass' Paper;" Frederick Douglass, Editor.

A number of gentlemen have been authors of narratives, written by themselves, some of which are masterly efforts, manifesting great force of talents. Of such, are those by Frederick Douglass, William Wells Brown, and Henry Bibb.

Of the various churches and clergy we have nothing to say, as these do not come within our province; except where individuals, from position, come within the sphere of our arrangement.

There have been several inventors among the colored people. The youth Henry Blair, of Maryland, some years ago, invented the Corn-Planter, and Mr. Roberts of Philadelphia, 1842, a machine for lifting cars off the railways.

It may be expected that we should say something about a book issued in Boston, purporting to be a history of ancient great men of African descent, by one Mr. Lewis, entitled "Light and Truth." This book is nothing more than a compilation of selected portions of Rollin's, Goldsmith's, Furguson's, Hume's, and other ancient histories; added to which, is a tissue of historical absurdities and literary blunders, shamefully palpable, for which the author or authors should mantle their faces.

If viewed in the light of a "Yankee trick," simply by which to

Hale, United States Senator, and after leaving College as his first public act, commenced the publication of a newspaper, for the elevation of colored Americans, called "Freedom's Journal." Subsequently to the publication of his paper, Mr. Russworm became interested in the Colonization scheme, then in its infancy, and went to Liberia; after which he went to Bassa Cove, of which place he was made governor, where he died in 1851.

make money, it may, peradventure, be a very clever trick; but the publisher should have recollected, that the ostensible object of his work was, the edification and enlightenment of the public in general and the colored people in particular, upon a great and important subject of truth; and that those who must be the most injured by it, will be the very class of people, whom he professes a desire to benefit. We much regret the fact, that there are but too many of our brethren, who undertake to dabble in literary matters, in the shape of newspaper and book-making, who are wholly unqualified for the important work. This, however, seems to be called forth by the palpable neglect, and indifference of those who have had the educational advantages, but neglected to make such use of them.

There is one redeeming quality about "Light and Truth." It is a capital offset to the pitiable literary blunders of Professor George R. Gliddon, late Consul to Egypt, from the United States, Lecturer on Ancient Egyptian Literature, &c., &c., who makes all ancient black men, *white;* and asserts the Egyptians and Ethiopians to have been of the *Caucasian* or white race!—So, also, this colored gentleman, makes all ancient great white men, *black*—as Diogenes, Socrates, Themistocles, Pompey, Cæsar, Cato, Cicero, Horace, Virgil, et cetera. Gliddon's idle nonsense has found a capital match in the production of Mr. Lewis' "Light and Truth," and both should be sold together. We may conclude by expressing our thanks to our brother Lewis, as we do not think that Professor Gliddon's learned ignorance, would have ever met an equal but for "Light and Truth." Reverends D. A. Payne, M. M. Clark, and other learned colored gentlemen, agree with us in the disapproval of this book.—EDITOR.

Benjamin Coker, a colored Methodist clergyman, forty years ago, wrote and issued, in the city of Baltimore, Maryland, a pamphlet, setting forth in glowing terms, the evils of American slavery, and the wrongs inflicted on the colored race. Rev. Daniel A. Payne, a talented clergyman, mentioned in this work, has now in his possession a copy of the pamphlet, and informs us, that the whole ground assumed by the modern abolitionists, was taken and reviewed in this pamphlet, by Daniel Coker. We may reasonably infer, that the ideas of Anti-Slavery, as taught by the friends of the black race at the present day, were borrowed from Mr. Coker; though, perhaps, policy forbade due credit to the proper source. Coker, like Russworm, became interested in the cause of African Colonization, and went to Africa; where he subsequently became an extensive coast trader, having several vessels, one of which he commanded in person, taking up his residence on the island of Sherbro, where he is said to have lived in great splendor. He died in 1845 or 1846, at an advanced age, leaving a family of sons and daughters.

Henry Bibb, an eloquent speaker, for several years, was the principal traveling lecturer for the Liberty Party of Michigan. Mr. Bibb, with equal advantages, would equal many of those who fill high places in the country, and now assume superiority over him and his kindred. He fled an exile from the United States, in 1850, to Canada, to escape the terrible consequences of the Republican Fugitive Slave Law, which threatened him with a total destruction of liberty. Mr. Bibb established the "Voice of the Fugitive," a newspaper, in Sandwich, Canada West, which is managed and conducted with credit.

Titus Basfield, graduated at Franklin College, New Athens, Ohio, receiving his religious instruction from the late Dr. Jonathan Walker, of that place, a physician and Covenanter clergyman. He afterwards graduated in theology at the Theological Seminary of Cannonsburg, Pennsylvania, was ordained, and traveled preaching and lecturing to the people of his peculiar faith and the public, for several years. He went to New London, Canada West, where he has charge of a Scotch congregation of religious votaries to that ancient doctrine of salvation.

Mary Ann Shadd, a very intelligent young lady, peculiarly eccentric, published an excellent pamphlet, issued from the press in Wilmington, Delaware, in 1849, on the elevation of the colored people. The writer of this work, was favored with an examination of it before publication, which he then highly approved of, as an excellent introduction to a great subject, fraught with so much interest. Miss Shadd has traveled much, and now has charge of a school in Sandwich, Canada West.

James McCrummill, of Philadelphia, is a skillful surgeon-dentist, and manufacturer of porcelain teeth, having practised the profession for many years in that city. He is said to be equal to the best in the city, and probably only requires an undivided attention to establish the reality.

Joseph Wilson, Thomas Kennard, and William

Nickless, are also practising dentists in the city of Philadelphia. Mr. Kennard is said to be one of the best *workmen* in the manufacture of artificial teeth, and *gums*—a new discovery, and very valuable article, in this most beautiful and highly useful art. He devotes several hours a day, to the manufacture of these articles for one of the principal surgeon-dentists of Arch street.

James M. Whitfield, of Buffalo, New York, though in an humble position, (for which we think he is somewhat reprehensible,) is one of the purest poets in America. He has written much for different news-papers; and, by industry and application—being already a good English scholar—did he but place himself in a favorable situation in life, would not be second to John Greenleaf Whittier, nor the late Edgar A. Poe.

Mary Elizabeth Miles, in accordance with the established rules, graduated as a teacher, in the Normal School, at Albany, New York, several years ago. Miss Miles (now Mrs. Bibb) was a very talented young lady and successful teacher. She spent several years of usefulness in Massachusetts, and Philadelphia, Pennsylvania, after which she went to Cincinnati, as assistant-teacher in Gilmore's "High School for Colored Children," which ended her public position in life. She now resides in Sandwich, Canada West.

Lucy Stanton, of Columbus, Ohio, is a graduate of Oberlin Collegiate Institute, in that State. She is now engaged in teaching school in that city, in which she is reputed to be successful. She is quite a young lady, and has her promise of life all before her, and bids fair to become a woman of much usefulness in society.

Doctor Bias, of Philadelphia, spoken of in another place, graduated at the close of the session of 1851–52, in the Eclectic Medical College, in that city. The doctor is highly esteemed by the physicians of his system, who continually interchange calls with him. He is also a practical phrenologist,—which profession he does not now attend to, giving his undivided attention to the practice of medicine,—and has written a pamphlet on that subject, entitled, " Synopsis of Phrenology, and the Phrenological Developments, as given by J. J. Gould Bias." No man perhaps, in the community of Philadelphia, possesses more self-will, and determination of character, than Dr. James Joshua Gould Bias. Mr. Whipper says of him, that he is " a Napoleon in character." The sterling trait in his character is, that he grasps after *originality*, and grapples with every difficulty. Such a man, must and will succeed in his undertakings.

CHAPTER XII.

STUDENTS OF VARIOUS PROFESSIONS.

THERE are a number of young gentlemen who have finished their literary course, who are now studying for the different learned professions, in various parts of the country.

Jonathan Gibbs, A. B., a very talented young gentleman, and fine speaker, is now finishing his professional studies in the Theological School at Dartmouth University. Mr. Gibbs also studied in the Scientific Department of the same Institution.

William H. Day, Esq., A. B., a graduate of Oberlin Collegiate Institute, is now in Cleveland Ohio, preparing for the Bar. Mr. Day is, perhaps, the most eloquent young gentleman of his age in the United States.

John Mercer Langston, A. B., of Chillicothe, Ohio, also a graduate of Oberlin College, a talented young gentleman, and promising orator, is completing a Theological course at the School of Divinity at Oberlin. It is said, that Mr. Langston intends also to prepare for the Bar. He commenced the study of Law previous to that of Theology, under Judge Andrews of Cleveland.

Charles Dunbar, of New York city, a promising, very intelligent young gentleman, is now in the office of Dr. Childs, and having attended one course of Lec-

tures at Bowdoin Medical School in Maine, will finish
next fall and winter, for the practice of his profession.
Isaac Humphrey Snowden, a promising young gentleman of talents, is now reading Medicine under Dr.
Clarke of Boston, and attended the session of the
Medical School of Harvard University, of 1850–'51.
Daniel Laing, Jr., Esq., a fine intellectual young
gentleman of Boston, a student also of Dr. Clarke of
that city, one of the Surgeons of the Massachusetts
General Hospital, who attended the course of Lectures the session of 1850–'51, at the Medical School
of Harvard University, is now in Paris, to spend two
years in the hospitals, and attend the Medical Lectures of that great seat of learning. Mr. Laing, like
most medical students, has ever been an admirer, and
anxious to sit under the teachings of that great master
in Surgery, Velpeau.

Dr. James J. Gould Bias, a Botanic Physician, and
talented gentleman of Philadelphia, is a member of the
class of 1851–'52, of the Eclectic Medical School of
that city. Dr. Bias deserves the more credit for his
progress in life, as he is entirely self-made.

Robert B. Leach, of Cleveland, Ohio, a very intelligent young gentleman, is a member of the medical
class for 1851–2, of the Homeopathic College, in that
City. Mr. Leach, when graduated, will be the *First
Colored Homeopathic* Physician in the United States.

Dr. John Degrass, of New York city, named in
another place, spent two years in Paris Hospitals,
under the teaching of the great lecturer and master of
surgery, Velpeau, to whom he was assistant and dres-

ser, in the hospital—the first position—for advantages, held by a student. The Doctor has subsequently been engaged as surgeon on a Havre packet, where he discharged the duties of his office with credit.

Also Dr. Peter Ray, of Brooklyn, named on the same page, graduated at Castleton Medical School, Vermont, spent some time at the Massachusetts General Hospital, Boston, where he held the position of assistant and dresser to Surgeon Parkman, in his ward of the hospital.

Dr. John P. Reynolds, has for a number of years been one of the most popular and successful physicians in Vincennes, Indiana. We believe Dr. Reynolds, was not of the "regular" system, but some twenty-three or four years ago, studied under an "Indian physician," after which, he practised very successfully in Zanesville, Ohio, subsequently removing to Vincennes, where he has for the last sixteen years, supported an enviable reputation as a physician. We understand Doctor Reynolds has entered into all the scientific improvements of the "eclectic school" of medicine, which has come into being in the United States, long since his professional career commenced. His popularity is such, that he has frequently been entrusted, with public confidence, and on one occasion, in 1838, was appointed by the court, sole executor of a very valuable orphans' estate. The Doctor has grown quite wealthy it is said, commanding a considerable influence in the community.

Dr. McDonough, a skillful young physician, graduated at the Institute, Easton, Pennsylvania, and finished his medical education at the University of New York. The Doctor is one of the most thorough of the young physicians; has been attached to the greater part of the public institutions of the city of New York, and is a good practical chemist.

Of course, there are many others, but as we have taken no measures whatever, to collect facts or information from abroad, only getting such as was at hand, and giving the few sketches here, according to our own recollection of them, we close this short chapter at this point.

CHAPTER XIII.

A SCAN AT PAST THINGS.

IT may not be considered in good taste to refer to those still living, who formerly occupied prominent business positions, and by dint of misfortune or fortune, have withdrawn. Nevertheless, we shall do so, since our simple object in this hasty sketch of things, is to show that the colored people of the country have not as has been charged upon them, always been dregs on the community and excrescences on the body politic, wherever they may have lived. We only desire to show that they have been, all things considered, just like other people.

Several years ago, there lived in the city of St.

Louis, Missouri, Mr. Berry Mechum. This gentleman was very wealthy, and had at one time, two fine steamers plying on the Mississippi, all under the command and management of white men, to whom he trusted altogether. As late as 1836, he sent two sons to the Oberlin Collegiate Institute, desiring that they might become educated, in order to be able to manage his business; who, although he could read and write, was not sufficiently qualified and skilled in the arts of business to vie with the crafty whites of the Valley. But before his sons were fitted for business, though reputed very wealthy, which there is no doubt he was, his whole property was seized and taken: and as he informed the writer himself, he did not know what for, as he had no debts that he knew of, until these suits were entered.   Mr. Mechum was an energetic, industrious, persevering old gentleman— a baptist clergyman, and published a small pamphlet on the condition of the colored race.   And although, it evinces great deficiency of literary qualifications, yet, does credit to the good old man, for the sound thoughts therein contained.

Also in the city of St. Louis, David Desara, who was a Mississippi pilot for many years. He made much money at his business, and owned at one time, a steamboat, which he piloted himself. Mr. Desara also failed, in consequence of having his business all in the hands of white men, as most of the slave state colored people have, entrusting to them entirely, without knowing anything of their own concerns.

Charles Moore, long and familiarly known as

" Charley Moore the Pilot," was for many years, one
of the most popular pilots on the Ohio and Mississippi rivers. Mr. Moore made much money, and with-
drew from his old business, purchasing a large tract
of land in Mercer County, Ohio, where he has for the
last ten or twelve years been farming.

Mr. Moore was an honest man, and we believe upon
him originated the purely Western phrase, "Charley
Moore the fair thing;" he always in his dealings saying " gentlemen, do the *fair* thing."

Abner H. Francis and James Garrett were formerly extensive clothes dealers in Buffalo, N. Y.,
doing business to the amount of sixty thousand dollars annually. They were energetic, industrious, persevering gentlemen, commencing business under very
unfavorable circumstances, in fact, commencing on
but *seventy-five* dollars, as the writer has been authentically informed by the parties.

They continued successfully for years, where their
paper and endorsements were good for any amount
they wanted—highly respected and esteemed ; Mr.
Francis sitting at one time as juryman in the court of
quarter sessions. These gentlemen failed in business
in 1849, but since then, have nearly adjusted the
claims against them. Mr. Francis has since settled
in Oregon Territory, Portland City, where he is again
doing a fair mercantile business. They bid fair again
to rank among the " merchant princes" of the times.

Robert Banks was for many years, a highly esteemed and extensive clothes dealer, on Jefferson
Avenue, in Detroit, Mich. No man was more highly

respected for unswerving integrity, and uprightness
of purpose, than Robert Banks, of Detroit.   Mr.
Banks, had much enlarged his business, immediately
succeeding a fire in which he was burnt out two
years previous to closing, which ensued in July, 1851,
being the second time he had lost his store by fire.
He might have, had he done as merchants usually do
under such circumstances, continued his business; but
instead, he made an assignment, with few preferred
creditors, rather as he expressed it, ruin his business,
than wilfully wrong a creditor. What speaks volumes
in his behalf, every person, even his greatest creditors
say, " He is an honest man ;" and while settling the
business of the late concern, those to whom he was indebted, offered him assistance to commence business
again.   But this he thankfully declined, preferring to
take his chance with others in the land of gold, California, where he now is, than commence again under
the circumstances.   Doubtless, if no special preven-
tion ensue, Mr. Banks will be fully able to redeem his
present obligations, and once more be found prospering and happy.

Henry Knight, of Chicago, commenced business in
that city without capital; but by industry, soon
gained the esteem and confidence of the public,
making many friends.   He fast rose in prosperity,
until he became the proprietor of the most extensive
livery establishment in the city, in which he had much
capital invested.   Determined to be equal to the
times, the growing prosperity of the city, and the
demands of the increasing pride of the place, he ex-

tended his possessions—erecting costly buildings, besides increasing his stock and livery extensively. He
was burnt out—a pressure came upon him—he sold
out his stock, staid suits against himself; went to California, returned in a year and a half—paid off old
claims, saved his property—went back; opened a California hotel, returned in less than one year with several thousand dollars, and now stands entirely clear of
all debt—and all this done in the space of two and a
half years. Mr. Knight is a man of business, and
will hold his position with others if he have but half
a chance. With such a man, there is "no such a
thing as fail"—he could not again, if he desired, because, his friends would not permit him.

CHAPTER XIV.

LATE MEN OF LITERARY, PROFESSIONAL AND ARTISTIC NOTE.

LATE Captain Frank Johnson, of Philadelphia, the
most renowned band leader ever known in the United
States, was a man of science, and master of his profession. In 1838, Captain Johnson went to England
with his noble band of musicians, where he met with
great success—played to Her Majesty Queen Victo-
ria and His Royal Highness Prince Albert—Captain
Johnson receiving a handsome French bugle, by order

of her Majesty, valued at five hundred dollars—
returning, he held throughout the Eastern, Northern,
and Western States, grand concerts, known as
" Soirees Musicales." He was a great composer
and teacher of music, and some of the finest Marches
and Cotillions now extant, have been originally composed by Captain Frank Johnson. On his Western
tour, by some awkwardness of management, he lost
at Buffalo, original music in manuscript, which never
had been published—as much of his composition had
been; valued at one thousand dollars, which, although
advertised, he never got. But his name was sufficient to give additional value to the prize; and there
is no doubt, but the world is now being benefited by
the labors of Captain Johnson, the credit being given
to others than himself. This was an unfortunate circumstance, and had his amiable and excellent widow,
Mrs. Helen Johnson of Philadelphia, now this composition, she could support herself in ease, by the sale
of the published work. Captain Frank Johnson,
died in Philadelphia in 1844, universally respected,
and regretted as an irreparable loss to society. At
his death the band divided, different members taking
a leadership.

Andrew J. Conner, one of the members of Captain
Johnson's band, also became a distinguished composer and teacher of music. Mr. Conner taught the
piano forte in the best families in the city of Philadelphia—among merchants, bankers, and professional
men. He contributed to the popular literary Maga-
zines of the day, and very many who have read in

Graham's and other literary issues, "Music composed by A. J. Conner," did not for a moment think that the author was a colored gentleman. Mr. Conner died in Philadelphia in 1850.

James Ulett, formerly of New York, became quite celebrated a few years since, as a comedian. He played several times in the old "Richmond Hill" Theatre, and quite successfully in Europe. Mr. Ulett was not well educated, and consequently, labored under considerable inconvenience in reading, frequently making grammatical blunders, as the writer noticed in a private rehearsal, in 1836, in the city of New York. He, however, possessed great intellectual powers, and his success depended more upon that, than his accuracy in reading. Of course, he was a great delineator of character, which being the principal feature in a comedian, his language was lost sight of in common conversation. Mr. Ulett died in New York a few years ago.

Doctor Lewis G. Wells was a most talented orator and man of literary qualifications. Residing in Baltimore, Maryland, he raised himself high in the estimation of all who knew him. He studied medicine, and was admitted into the Washington Medical College, attending the regular courses, and would have graduated, but for some misunderstanding between himself and the professors, which prevented it. He was a most successful practitioner, and effected more cures during the prevalence of the cholera in 1832, than any other physician in the city. Doctor Wells was also a most successful practical phrenologist, and lectured to large and fashionable houses of the first class ladies and gentlemen of Baltimore, and other cities. Being a great wit, he kept his audiences in uproars of laughter. Mr. Wells was also an ordained minister of the Gospel, belonging to the white Methodist connexion; and was author of several productions, among them, a large Methodist hymn book, containing several fine original poems. Dr. Wells died the same year of cholera, after successfully saving many others, because there was no physician at that time who understood the treatment of the disease.

———◦●◦———

CHAPTER XV.

FARMERS AND HERDSMEN.

LITTLE need be said about farmers; there are hundreds of them in all parts of the country, especially in the Western States; still these may not be considered of a conspicuous or leading character— albeit, they are contributing largely to the wants of community, and wealth of the country at large. Ohio, Michigan, Wisconsin, Iowa, Illinois, and Indiana, all, are largely represented by the farming interests of colored men. We shall name but a sufficient number to show the character of their enterprise in this department of American industry.

Rev. William Watson, of Cincinnati, Ohio, is the owner of a fine farm in Mercer county, and six hundred acres of additional land.

Mr. Richard Phillips, of the same city, is owner of a fine farm in the same county, and three hundred and fifty additional acres of land.

Rev. Reuben P. Graham, of Cincinnati, owns a finely cultivated farm in Mercer county, three hundred acres of adjoining land; and one near Cincinnati.

Mr. John Woodson, of Jackson county, is one of the most successful farmers in the State of Ohio. Having a large tract of land, he has one of the best cultivated farms in the West, in a most productive state, raising grains, fruits, and live-stock. In the year 1842, his farm produced that season, three thousand bushels of wheat, several hundred bushels of rye, eleven hundred bushels of oats, large crops of corn, potatoes, and other vegetables ; large quantities of fruits, three hundred stacks of hay, with a large stock of several hundred heads of cattle on the place. Mr. Woodson has for many years, been a highly respectable man in his neighborhood, and continues his farming interests with unabated success.

Dr. Charles Henry Langston, of Columbus, Ohio, is also the proprietor of a very fine farm of eleven hundred acres, in Jackson county, upon which he has a white tenant. This gentleman is a surgeon-dentist by profession, educated at Oberlin College, making his home in Columbus.

Robert Purvis, Esq., a gentleman of collegiate education, is proprietor of one of the best improved

farms in Philadelphia county, fifteen miles from Philadelphia.   His cattle consist of the finest English
breed.

Joseph Purvis, Esq., of Bucks county, Pennsylvania, a gentleman also of education and wealth, is
an amateur stock farmer.   Every animal on Mr.
Purvis' farm is of the very best breed—Godolphin
horses, Durham cattle, Leicestershire sheep, Berk-
shire swine, even English bull-terrier dogs, and whatever else pertains to the blooded breeds of brutes,
may be found on the farm of Joseph Purvis.   Mr.
Purvis supplies a great many farmers with choice
breeds of cattle, and it is said that he spends ten
thousand dollars annually, in the improvement of
his stocks.

Robert Briges Forten, also of Bucks county, Pennsylvania, is an amateur farmer.   Mr. Forten is a
gentleman of fine education, a pure, chaste poet, and
attends to farming for the love of nature.   He is a
valuable member of the farming enterprise in the
country.

If such evidence of industry and interest, as has
been exhibited in the various chapters on the different
pursuits and engagements of colored Americans, do
not entitle them to equal rights and privileges in
our common country, then indeed, is there nothing
to justify the claims of any portion of the American
people to the common inheritance of Liberty.

We proceed to another view of our condition in the
United States.

CHAPTER XVI.

NATIONAL DISFRANCHISEMENT OF COLORED PEOPLE.

WE give below the Act of Congress, known as the "Fugitive Slave Law," for the benefit of the reader, as there are thousands of the American people of all classes, who have never read the provisions of this enactment; and consequently, have no conception of its enormity. We had originally intended, also, to have inserted here, the Act of Congress of 1793, but since this Bill includes all the provisions of that Act, in fact, although called a "supplement," is a substitute, *de facto*, it would be superfluous; therefore, we insert the Bill alone, with explanations following :—

AN ACT

To AMEND, AND SUPPLEMENTARY TO THE ACT, ENTITLED, " AN ACT RESPECTING FUGITIVES FROM JUSTICE, AND PERSONS ESCAPING FROM THE SERVICE OF THEIR MASTERS," APPROVED FEBRUARY 12, 1793.

Be it enacted by the Senate and House of Representatives of the United States of America in Congress assembled, That the persons who have been, or may hereafter be, appointed commissioners, in virtue of any act of Congress, by the circuit courts of the United States, and who, in consequence of such appointment, are authorized to exercise the powers that any justice of the peace or other magistrate of any of the United States may exercise in respect to offenders for any crime or offence against the United States, by arresting, imprisoning, or bailing the same under and by virtue of the thirty-third section of the act of the twenty-fourth of September, seventeen hundred and eighty-nine, entitled " An act to establish the judicial courts of the United States," shall be, and are hereby authorized and required to exercise and discharge all the powers and duties conferred by this act.

SEC. 2. *And be it further enacted,* That the superior court of each organized territory of the United States shall have the same power to appoint commissioners to take acknowledgements of bail and affidavit, and to take depositions of witnesses in civil causes, which is now possessed by the circuit courts of the United States; and all commissioners who shall hereafter be appointed for such purposes by the superior court of any organized territory of the United States shall possess all the powers and exercise all the duties conferred by law upon the commissioners appointed by the circuit courts of the United States for similar purposes, and shall moreover exercise and discharge all the powers and duties conferred by this act.

SEC. 3. *And be it further enacted,* That the circuit courts of the United States, and the superior courts of each organized territory of the United States, shall from time to time enlarge the number of commissioners, with a view to afford reasonable facilities to reclaim fugitives from labor, and to the prompt discharge of the duties imposed by this act.

SEC. 4. *And be it further enacted,* That the commissioners above named shall have concurrent jurisdiction with the judges of the circuit and district courts of the United States, in their respective circuits and districts within the several States, and the judges of the superior courts of the Territories, severally and collectively, in term time and vacation; and shall grant certificates to such claimants, upon satisfactory proof being made, with authority to take and remove such fugitives from service or labor, under the restrictions herein contained. to the State or territory from which such persons may have escaped or fled.

SEC. 5. *And be it further enacted,* That it shall be the duty of all marshals and deputy marshals to obey and execute all warrants and precepts issued under the provisions of this act, when to them directed; and should any marshal or deputy marshal refuse to receive such warrant or other process, when tendered, or to use all proper means diligently to execute the same, he shall, on conviction thereof, be fined in the sum of one thousand dollars to the use of such claimant, on the motion of such claimant, by the circuit or district court for the district of such marshal; and after arrest of such fugitive by such marshal or his deputy, or whilst at any time in his custody, under the provisions of this act, should such fugitive escape, whether with or without the assent of such marshal or his deputy, such marshal shall be liable, on his official bond, to be prosecuted, for the benefit of such claimant for the full value of the service or labor of said fugitive in the State, Territory, or district whence he escaped; and the better to enable the said commissioners, when thus appointed, to execute their duties faithfully and efficiently, in conformity with the requirements of the constitution of the United States and of this act, they are hereby authorized and empowered, within their counties respectively, to appoint in writing under their hands, any one or more suitable persons, from time to time, to execute all such warrants and other process as may be issued by them in the lawful performance of their respective duties; with an authority to such commissioners, or the persons to be appointed by them, to execute process as aforesaid, to summon and call to their aid the bystanders, or *posse comitatus* of the proper county, when necessary to insure a faithful observance of the clause of the constitution referred to, in conformity with the provisions of this act: and all good citizens are hereby commanded to aid and assist in the prompt and efficient execution of this law, whenever their services may be required, as aforesaid, for that person; and said warrants shall run and be executed by said officers anywhere in the State within which they are issued.

Sec. 6. *And be it further enacted,* That when a person held to service or labor in any State or Territory of the United States has heretofore or shall hereafter escape into another State or Territory of the United States, the person or persons to whom such service or labor may be due, or his, her, or their agent or attorney, duly authorized, by power of attorney, in writing, acknowledged and certified under the seal of some legal office or court of the State or Territory in which the same may be executed, may pursue and reclaim such fugitive person, either by procuring a warrant from some one of the courts, judges, or commissioners aforesaid, of the proper circuit, district or county, for the apprehension of such fugitive from service or labor, or by seizing and arresting such fugitive, where the same can be done without process, and by taking and causing such person to be taken forthwith before such court, judge or commissioner, whose duty it shall

be to hear and determine the case of such claimant in a summary
manner; and upon satisfactory proof being made, by deposition or
affidavit, in writing, to be taken and certified by such court, judge, or
commissioner, or by other satisfactory testimony, duly taken and
certified by some court, magistrate, justice of the peace, or other legal
officer authorized to administer an oath, and take depositions under
the laws of the State or Territory from which such person owing
service or labor may have escaped, with a certificate of such magistracy or other authority, as aforesaid, with the seal of the proper court
or officer thereto attached, which seal shall be sufficient to establish
the competency of the proof, and with proof, also by affidavit, of the
identity of the person whose service or labor is claimed to be due as
aforesaid, that the person so arrested does in fact owe service or labor
to the person or persons claiming him or her, in the State or Territory
from which such fugitive may have escaped as aforesaid, and that said
person escaped, to make out and deliver to such claimant, his or her
agent or attorney, a certificate setting forth the substantial facts as to
the service or labor due from such fugitive to the claimant, and
of his or her escape from the State or Territory in which such service
or labor was due to the State or Territory in which he or she was
arrested, with authority to such claimant, or his or her agent or attorney
to use such reasonable force and restraint as may be necessary under
the circumstances of the case, to take and remove such fugitive person back to the State or Territory from whence he or she may have
escaped as aforesaid. In no trial or hearing under this act shall the
testimony of such alleged fugitive be admitted in evidence; and the
certificates in this and the first section mentioned shall be conclusive
of the right of the person or persons in whose favor granted to remove
such fugitive to the State or Territory from which he escaped, and shall
prevent all molestation of said person or persons by any process issued
by any court, judge, magistrate, or other person whomsoever.

Sec. 7. *And be it further enacted*, That any person who shall
knowingly and willingly obstruct, hinder, or prevent such claimant,
his agent or attorney, or any person or persons lawfully assisting him,
her, or them, from arresting such a fugitive from service or labor,
either with or without process as aforesaid; or shall rescue, or attempt
to rescue such fugitive from service or labor, from the custody of such
claimant, his or her agent or attorney or other person or persons law-

fully assisting as aforesaid, when so arrested, pursuant to the authority herein given and declared: or shall aid, abet, or assist such person, so owing service or labor as aforesaid, directly or indirectly, to escape from such claimant, his agent or attorney, or other person or persons, legally authorized as aforesaid ; or shall harbor or conceal such fugitive, so as to prevent the discovery and arrest of such person, after notice or knowledge of the fact that such person was a fugitive from service or labor as aforesaid, shall, for either of said offences, be subject to a fine not exceeding one thousand dollars, and imprisonment not exceeding six months, by indictment and conviction before the district court of the United States for the district in which such offence may have been committed, or before the proper court of criminal jurisdiction, if committed within any one of the organized territories of the United States ; and shall moreover forfeit and pay, by way of civil damages to the party injured by such illegal conduct, the sum of one thousand dollars for each fugitive so lost as aforesaid, to be recovered by action of debt in any of the district or territorial courts aforesaid, within whose jurisdiction the said offence may have been committed.

Sec. 8. *And be it further enacted*, That the marshals, their deputies, and the clerks of the said district and territorial courts, shall be paid for their services the like fees as may be allowed to them for similar services in other cases; and where such services are rendered exclusively in the arrest, custody, and delivery of the fugitive to the claimant, his or her agent or attorney, or where such supposed fugitive may be discharged out of custody for the want of sufficient proof as aforesaid, then such fees are to be paid in the whole by such claimant, his agent or attorney ; and in all cases where the proceedings are before a commissioner, he shall be entitled to a fee of ten dollars in full for his services in each case, upon delivery of the said certificate to the claimant, his or her agent or attorney ; or a fee of five dollars in cases where the proof shall not, in the opinion of such commissioner, warrant such certificate and delivery, inclusive of all services incident to such arrest and examination, to be paid in either case, by the claimant, his or her agent or attorney. The person or persons authorized to execute the process to be issued by such commissioners for the arrest and detention of fugitives from service or labor as aforesaid, shall also be entitled to a fee of five dollars each for each person he or they may arrest and take before any such commissioner as aforesaid at the instance and request of such claimant, with such other fees as may be deemed reasonable by such commissioner for such other additional services as may be necessarily performed by him or them : such as attending to the examination, keeping the fugitive in custody, and providing him with food and lodging during his detention, and until the final determination of such commissioner ; and in general for performing such other duties as may be required by such claimant, his or her attorney or agent, or commissioner in the premises ; such fees to be made up in conformity with the fees usually charged by the officers of the courts of justice within the proper district or county, as near as may be practicable, and paid by such claimants, their agents or attorneys, whether such supposed fugitive from service or labor be ordered to be delivered to such claimants by the final·determination of such commissioners or not.

Sec. 9. *And be it further enacted*, That upon affidavit made by the claimant of such fugitive, his agent or attorney, after such certificate has been issued, that he has reason to apprehend that such fugitive will be rescued by force from his or their possession before he can be taken beyond the limits of the State in which the arrest is made, it shall be the duty of the officer making the arrest to retain such fugitive in his custody, and to remove him to the State whence he fled, and there to deliver him to said claimant, his agent or attorney. And to this end the officer aforesaid is hereby authorized and required to employ so many persons as he may deem necessary, to overcome such force, and to retain them in his service so long as circumstances may require ; the said officer and his assistants, while so employed, to receive the same compensation, and to be allowed the same expenses as are now allowed by law for the transportation of criminals, to be certified by the judge of the district within which the arrest is made, and paid out of the treasury of the United States.

Sec. 10. *And be it further enacted*, That when any person held to service or labor in any State or Territory, or in the District of Columbia, shall escape therefrom, the party to whom such service or labor shall be due, his, her, or their agent or attorney may apply to any court of record therein, or judge thereof, in vacation, and make satisfactory proof to such court, or judge, in vacation, of the escape aforesaid, and that the person escaping owed service or labor to such party.

Whereupon the court shall cause a record to be made of the matters so proved, and also a general description of the person so escaping, with such convenient certainty as may be ; and a transcript of such record authenticated by the attestation of the clerk, and of the seal of the said court, being produced in any other State, Territory, or District in which the person so escaping may be found, and being exhibited to any judge, commissioner, or other officer, authorized by the law of the United States to cause persons escaping from service or labor to be delivered up, shall be held and taken to be full and conclusive evidence of the fact of escape, and that the service or labor of the person escaping is due to the party in such record mentioned. And upon the production by the said party of other and further evidence, if necessary, either oral or by affidavit, in addition to what is contained in the said record of the identity of the person escaping, he or she shall be delivered up to the claimant. And the said court, commissioner, judge or other person authorized by this act to grant certificates to claimants of fugitives, shall, upon the production of the record and other evidences aforesaid, grant to such claimant a certificate of his right to take any such person identified and proved to be owing service or labor as aforesaid, which certificate shall authorize such claimant to seize or arrest and transport such person to the State or Territory from which he escaped : *Provided*, That nothing herein contained shall be construed as requiring the production of a transcript of such record as evidence as aforesaid ; but in its absence, the claim shall be heard and determined upon other satisfactory proofs competent in law.

HOWELL COBB,
Speaker of the House of Representatives.
WILLIAM R. KING,
President of the Senate, pro tempore.
Approved September 18, 1850.
MILLARD FILLMORE.

The most prominent provisions of the Constitution of the United States, and those which form the fundamental basis of personal security, are they which provide, that every person shall be secure in their person and property : that no person may be deprived of liberty without due process of law, and that for crime or misdemeanor ; that there may be no process of law that shall work corruption of blood. By corruption of blood is meant, that process, by which a person is *degraded* and deprived of rights common to the enfranchised citizen—of the rights of an elector, and of eligibility to the office of a representative of the people; in a word, that no person nor their posterity, may ever be debased beneath the level of the recognised basis of American citizenship. This debasement and degradation is "corruption of blood;" politically understood—a legal acknowledgement of inferiority of birth.

Heretofore, it ever has been denied, that the United States recognised or knew any difference between the people—that the Constitution makes no distinction, but includes in its provisions, all the people alike. This is not true, and certainly is blind absurdity in us at least, who have suffered the dread consequences of this delusion, not now to see it.

By the provisions of this bill, the colored people of the United States are positively degraded beneath the level of the whites—are made liable at any time, in any place, and under all circumstances, to be arrested—and upon the claim of any white person, without the privilege, even of making a defence, sent into endless bondage. Let no visionary nonsense about *habeas corpus*, or a *fair trial*, deceive us ; there are no such rights granted in this bill, and except where the commissioner is too ignorant to understand when reading it, or too stupid to enforce it when he does understand, there is no earthly chance—no hope under heaven for the colored person who is brought before one of these officers of the law. Any leniency that may be expected, must proceed from the whims or caprice of the magistrate—in fact, it is optional with them; and *our* rights and liberty entirely at their disposal.

We are slaves in the midst of freedom, waiting patiently, and unconcernedly—indifferently, and stupidly, for masters to come and lay claim to us, trusting to their generosity, whether or not they will own us and carry us into endless bondage.

The slave is more secure than we; he knows who holds the heel upon his bosom—we know not the wretch who may grasp us by the throat. His master may be a man of some conscientious scruples; ours may be unmerciful. Good or bad, mild or harsh, easy or hard, lenient or severe, saint or satan—whenever that master demands any one of us—even our affectionate wives and darling little children, *we must go into slavery*—there is *no alternative*. The *will* of the man who sits in judgment on our liberty, is the law. To him is given *all power* to say, whether or not we have a right to enjoy freedom. This is the power over the slave in the South—this is now extended to the North. The will of the man who sits in judgment over us is the law; because it is explicitly provided that the *decision* of the commissioner shall be final, from which there can be no appeal.

The freed man of the South is even more secure

than the freeborn of the North; because such persons usually have their records in the slave states, bringing their "papers" with them; and the slaveholders will be faithful to their own acts. The Northern freeman knows no records; he despises the "papers."

Depend upon no promised protection of citizens in any quarter. Their own property and liberty are jeopardised, and they will not sacrifice them for us. This we may not expect them to do.

Besides, there are no people who ever lived, love their country and obey their laws as the Americans.

Their country is their Heaven—their Laws their Scriptures—and the decrees of their Magistrates obeyed as the fiat of God. It is the most consummate delusion and misdirected confidence to depend upon them for protection; and for a moment suppose even our children safe while walking in the streets among them.

A people capable of originating and sustaining such a law as this, are not the people to whom we are willing to entrust our liberty at discretion.

What can we do?—What shall we do? This is the great and important question :—Shall we submit to be dragged like brutes before heartless men, and sent into degradation and bondage?—Shall we fly, or shall we resist? Ponder well and reflect.

A learned jurist in the United States, (Chief Justice John Gibson of Pennsylvania,) lays down this as a fundamental right in the United States: that "Every man's house is his castle, and he has the right to defend it unto the taking of life, against any attempt to

enter it against his will, except for crime," by well
authenticated process.

But we have no such right. It was not intended
for us, any more than any other provision of the law,
intended for the protection of Americans. The policy
is against us—it is useless to contend against it.

This is the law of the land and must be obeyed;
and we candidly advise that it is useless for us to contend against it. To suppose its repeal, is to anticipate
an overthrow of the Confederative Union; and we
must be allowed an expression of opinion, when we
say, that candidly we believe, the existence of the Fugitive Slave Law *necessary* to the continuance of the
National Compact. This Law is the foundation of
the Compromise—remove it, and the consequences are
easily determined. We say necessary to the continuance of the National Compact: certainly we will
not be understood as meaning that the enactment of
such a Law was *really* necessary, or as favoring in the
least this political monstrosity of the THIRTY-FIRST
CONGRESS of the UNITED STATES of AMERICA—surely
not at all; but we speak logically and politically,
leaving morality and right out of the question—taking
our position on the acknowledged popular basis of
American Policy ; arguing from premise to conclusion.
We must abandon all vague theory, and look at *facts*
as they really are ; viewing ourselves in our true political position in the body politic. To imagine ourselves to be included in the body politic, except by
express legislation, is at war with common sense, and
contrary to fact. Legislation, the administration of

the laws of the country, and the exercise of rights by
the people, all prove to the contrary. We are politically, not of them, but aliens to the laws and political
privileges of the country. These are truths—fixed
facts, that quaint theory and exhausted moralising, are
impregnable to, and fall harmlessly before.

It is useless to talk about our rights in individual
States : we can have no rights there as citizens, not
recognised in our common country ; as the citizens of
one State, are entitled to all the rights and privileges
of an American citizen in all the States—the nullity
of the one necessarily implying the nullity of the
other. These provisions then do not include the colored
people of the United States ; since there is no power
left in them, whereby they may protect us as their
own citizens. Our descent, by the laws of the country, stamps us with inferiority—upon us has this law
worked *corruption of blood.* We are in the hands
of the General Government, and no State can rescue
us. The Army and Navy stand at the service of
our enslavers, the whole force of which, may at any
moment—even in the dead of night, as has been
done—when sunk in the depth of slumber, called out
for the purpose of forcing our mothers, sisters, wives,
and children, or ourselves, into hopeless servitude,
there to weary out a miserable life, a relief from
which, death would be hailed with joy. Heaven and
earth—God and Humanity !—are not these sufficient to
arouse the most worthless among mankind, of whatever descent, to a sense of their true position ? These
laws apply to us—shall we not be aroused ?

What then shall we do?—what is the remedy—is the important question to be answered?

This important inquiry we shall answer, and find a remedy in when treating of the emigration of the colored people.

———•———

CHAPTER XVII.

EMIGRATION OF THE COLORED PEOPLE OF THE UNITED STATES.

THAT there have been people in all ages under certain circumstances, that may be benefited by emigration, will be admitted; and that there are circumstances under which emigration is absolutely necessary to their political elevation, cannot be disputed.

This we see in the Exodus of the Jews from Egypt to the land of Judea; in the expedition of Dido and her followers from Tyre to Mauritania; and not to dwell upon hundreds of modern European examples— also in the ever memorable emigration of the Puritans, in 1620, from Great Britain, the land of their birth, to the wilderness of the New World, at which may be fixed the beginning of emigration to this continent as a permanent residence.

This may be acknowledged; but to advocate the emigration of the colored people of the United States from their native homes, is a new feature in our history, and at first view, may be considered objectionable, as pernicious to our interests. This objection is at once removed, when reflecting on our condition as incontrovertibly shown in a foregoing part of this work. And we shall proceed at once to give the advantages to be derived from emigration, to us as a people, in preference to any other policy that we may adopt. This granted, the question will then be, Where shall we go? This we conceive to be all-important—of paramount consideration, and shall endeavor to show the most advantageous locality; and premise the recommendation, with the strictest advice against any countenance whatever, to the emigration scheme of the so called Republic of Liberia.

CHAPTER XVIII.

"REPUBLIC OF LIBERIA."

THAT we desire the civilization and enlightenment of Africa—the high and elevated position of Liberia among the nations of the earth, may not be doubted, as the writer was among the first, seven or eight years ago, to make the suggestion and call upon the Liberians to hold up their heads like men; take courage, having confidence in their own capacity to govern themselves, and come out from their disparaging position, by formally declaring their Independence. As our desire is to impart information, and enlighten the minds of our readers on the various subjects herein contained, we present below a large extract from the "First Annual Report of the Trustees of Donations for Education in Liberia." This Extract will make a convenient statistic reference for matters concerning Liberia. We could only wish that many of our readers possessed more historical and geographical information of the world, and there could be little fears of their going anywhere that might be incongenial and unfavorable to their success. We certainly do intend to deal fairly with Liberia, and give the reader every information that may tend to enlighten them. What the colored people most need, is *intelligence ;* give them this, and there is no danger of them being duped into anything they do not desire. This Board was incorporated by the Legislature of Massachusetts, March 19th, 1850—Ensign H. Kellogg, Speaker of the House, Marshall P. Wilder, President of the Senate. Trustees of the Board—Hon. George N. Briggs, LL. D., Hon. Simon Greenleaf, LL. D., Hon. Stephen Fairbanks, Hon. William J. Hubbard, Hon. Joel Giles, Hon. Albert Fearing, Amos A. Lawrence, Esq. Officers of the Board—Hon. G. N. Briggs, President ; Hon. S. Fairbanks, Treasurer ; Rev. J. Tracy, Secretary. The conclusion of the Report says :—" In view of such considerations, the Trustees cannot doubt the patrons of learning will sustain them in their attempt to plant the FIRST COLLEGE on

the *only*-continent which yet remains *without* one."
In this, the learned Trustees have fallen into a statis-
tical and geographical error, which we design to correct.
The *continent* is *not without* a College. There are
now in Egypt, erected under the patronage of that
singularly wonderful man, Mehemet Ali, four colleges
conducted on the European principle—Scientific,
Medical, Legal, and Military.* These are in successful operation; the Military College having an
average of eleven hundred students annually. The
continent of Africa then, is not without a college, but
though benighted enough, even to an apparent hopeless degeneration, she is still the seat of learning, and
must some day rise, in the majesty of ancient grandeur,
and vindicate the rights and claims of her own children,
against the incalculable wrongs perpetrated through
the period of sixty ages by professedly enlightened
Christians, against them.

A glance at the map will show a sharp bend in this coast
at Cape Palmas, from which it extends, on the one side,
about 1,100 miles north-west and north, and on the other,
about 1,200 or 1,300 almost directly east. In this bend is
the Maryland Colony of Cape Palmas, with a jurisdiction
extending nearly 100 miles eastward. This Colony is
bounded on the north-west by the Republic of Liberia,
which extends along the coast about 400 miles to Sherbro.

* It may be, that the Medical and Legal Schools, are adjunct
departments of the Scientific College, which would make the number
of Colleges in Egypt but two : as we are certain that the Military is
separate entirely from the Scientific School, and spoken of by travelers as a splendid College.

These two governments will ultimately be united in one Republic, and may be considered as one, for all the purposes of this inquiry. The extent of their united sea-coast is about 520 miles. The jurisdiction of the Republic over the four hundred miles or more which it claims, has been formally acknowledged by several of the leading powers of Europe, and is questioned by none. To almost the whole of it, the native title has been extinguished; the natives, however, still occupying, as citizens, such portions of it as they need.

The civilized population of these governments, judging from the census of 1843, and other information, is some 7,000 or 8000. Of the heathen population, no census has ever been taken; but it probably exceeds 300,000.

The grade of Liberian civilization may be estimated from the fact, that the people have formed a republican government, and so administer it, as to secure the confidence of European governments in its stability. The native tribes who have merged themselves in the Republic, have all bound themselves to receive and encourage teachers; and some of them have insisted on the insertion, in their treaties of annexation, of pledges that teachers and other means of civilization shall be furnished.

Our accounts of churches, clergy and schools are defective, but show the following significant facts:

The clergy of the Methodist Episcopal Church in Liberia are nearly all Liberian citizens, serving as missionaries of the Methodist Missionary Society in the United States. The last Report of that Society gives the names of fifteen missionaries, having in charge nine circuits, in which are 882 members in full communion, and 235 probationers; total, 1,117. They have 20 Sabbath Schools, with 114 officers and teachers, 810 scholars, and 507 volumes in their

libraries. They have a Manual Labor School and Female
Academy. The number of Day Schools is not reported;
but seven of the missionaries are reported as superintend-
ents of schools, and the same number have under their
charge several " native towns," in some of which there are
schools. The late superintendent of the missions writes :—
" It appears plain to my mind, that nothing can now re-
tard the progress of our missions in this land, unless it be
the want of a good high school, in which to rear up an
abundant supply of well qualified teachers, to supply, as
they shall rapidly increase in number, all your schools."
    The Baptists are next in number to the Methodists.
The Northern Baptist Board, having its seat in Boston, has
in Liberia one mission, two out-stations, one boarding-
school, and two day schools, with about twenty scholars
each, one native preacher, and four native assistants. The
whole mission is in the hands of converted natives. The
Southern Board operates more extensively. More than
a year since, the Rev. John Day, its principal agent there,
reported to the Rev. R. R. Gurley, United States Commissioner to Liberia, as follows :
    " In our schools are taught, say, 330 children, 92 of
whom are natives. To more than 10,000 natives, the Word
of Life is statedly preached ; and in every settlement in
these colonies, we have a church, to whom the means of
grace are administered ; and in every village we have an
interesting Sunday school, where natives as well as colonists are taught the truths of God's word. Say, in our
Sunday schools, are taught 400 colonists, and 200 natives.
* * * * We have this year baptized 18 natives and 7
colonists, besides what have been baptized by Messrs. Mur-
ray and Drayton, from whom I have had no report."
    The missionaries are all, or nearly all, Liberian citizens.

The Board of Missions of the Presbyterian Church in the United States has five missionaries at four stations in Liberia. The first is at Monrovia, under the care of the Rev. Harrison W. Ellis, well known as "the Learned Black Blacksmith." While a slave in Alabama, and working at his trade as a blacksmith, he acquired all the education, in English, Latin, Greek, Hebrew, and Theology, which is required for ordination as a Presbyterian minister. The Presbyterians of that region then bought him, and sent him out as a missionary. His assistant, Mr. B. V. R. James, a colored man, was for some years a printer in the service of the American Board at their mission at Cape Palmas and the Gaboon River. He first went to Liberia as a teacher, supported by a society of ladies in New York. In the Presbyterian church under the care of Mr. Ellis are 39 communicants. During the year, 24 had been added, and 8 had been dismissed to form a new church in another place. Mr. Ellis also has charge of the "Alexander High School," which is intended mainly for teaching the rudiments of a classical education. This institution has an excellent iron school-house, given by a wealthy citizen of New York, at the cost of one thousand dollars, and a library and philosophical apparatus, which cost six hundred dollars, given by a gentleman in one of the southern States. The library contains a supply of classical works, probably equal to the wants of the school for some years. The land needed for the accommodation of the school was given by the government of Liberia. The number of scholars appears to be between twenty and thirty, a part of whom support themselves by their daily labor. The English High School under the care of Mr. James, had, according to the last Annual Report, 52 scholars. At a later date, the number in both schools was 78. Mr. James has also a large Sabbath school; but the number of pupils is not given.

The second station is at the new settlement of Kentucky, on the right or north bank of the St. Paul's, about fifteen miles from Monrovia, and six miles below Millsburgh. The missionary is a Liberian, Mr. H. W. Erskine. On a lot of ten acres, given by the government, buildings on an economical scale have been erected, in which is a school of twenty scholars. A church was organized in November, 1849, with eight members from the church in Monrovia. They have since increased to fourteen. Here, too, is a flourishing Sabbath school. The citizens, and especially the poor natives in the neighbourhood, are extremely anxious that a boarding school should be established. To this the Committee having charge of this mission objects, as the expense for buildings and for the support of pupils would be great, and would absorb funds that can be more profitably expended on day schools.

The third station is on the Sinou river, 150 miles down the coast from Monrovia, where, at the mouth of the river, is the town of Greenville, and a few miles higher up, the newer settlements of Readville and Rossville. It is under the care of the Rev. James M. Priest. The number of communicants, at the latest date, was thirty, and the field of labor was rapidly enlarging by immigration. The station is new, and it does not appear that any mission school had yet been organized.

The fourth station is at Settra Kroo, where there are five or six miles of coast, to which the native title has not yet been extinguished. This station has been maintained for some years, at a lamentable expense of the lives and health of white missionaries. About 200 boys and a few girls have been taught to read. The station is now under the care of Mr. Washington McDonogh, formerly a slave of the late John McDonogh, of Louisiana, so well known for the immense estate which he has bequeathed to benevolent purposes. He was well educated, and with more than eighty others, sent out some years since at his master's expense. He has a school of fifteen scholars, with the prospect of a large increase.

The mission of the Protestant Episcopal Church is located in the Maryland Colony at Cape Palmas. Its last Report specifies seven schools, and alludes to several others, in actual operation ; all containing from 200 to 300 scholars, of whom about 100 are in one Sabbath school. Five other schools had been projected, and have probably gone into operation since that time. The greater part of the pupils are from native families. The Report states the number of communicants at sixty-seven, of whom forty are natives. A High school was opened January 1, 1850.

The laws of the Republic of Liberia provide for a common school in every town. It is supposed, however, that where there is a mission school, accessible to all children of suitable age, no other school exists; so that, in fact, nearly all the common schools in Liberia are connected with the different missions, the missionaries have the superintendence of their studies, and the Missionary Societies defray a large portion of the expense. Yet it must be remembered that a large majority of the missionaries ere citizens of the Republic, and some of them native Africans ; so that the immediate control of the schools is not generally in foreign hands. A portion, also, of the missionary funds, is contributed in Liberia ; and something is paid by parents for the tuition of their children. Yet the Republic evidently needs an educational system more independent of missionary aid and control; and for that purpose, needs a supply of teachers who are not raised up in mission schools. And we have it in testimony, that the missions themselves might be more efficient for good, if well supplied with teachers of higher qualifications.

Here, then, we have a Republic of some 300,000 inhabitants, of whom 7,000 or 8,000 may be regarded as civilized, and the remainder as having a right to expect, and a large part of them actually expecting and demanding the means of civilization and Christianity. We have,—supplying as well as we can by estimate, the numbers not definitely given,—more than 2,000 communicants in Christian churches, and more than 1,500 children in Sabbath Schools; some 40 day schools containing, exclusive of the Methodists, who are the most numerous, and of whose numbers in school we have no report, about 635 scholars. The whole number in day schools, therefore, is probably not less than 1,200. We have the Alexander High School at Monrovia, where instruction is given to some extent in the classics; the English High School, at the same place, under Mr. James; the Methodist Manual Labor School and Female Academy at Millsburg; the Baptist Boarding School at Bexley; and the Protestant Episcopal High School at Cape Palmas. These institutions must furnish some students for a higher seminary, such as we propose to establish; and such a population must need their labors when educated.

However foreign to the designs of the writer of ever making that country or any other out of America, his home; had this been done, and honorably maintained, the Republic of Liberia would have met with words of encouragement, not only from himself, an humble individual, but we dare assert, from the leading spirits among, if not from the whole colored population of the United States. Because they would have been willing to overlook the circumstances under which they went there, so that in the end, they were willing to take their stand as men, and thereby throw off the degradation of slaves, still under the control of American slave-holders, and American slave-ships. But in this, we were disappointed—grievously disappointed, and proceed to show in short, our objections to Liberia.

Its geographical position, in the first place, is objectionable, being located in the *sixth degree* of latitude North of the equator, in a district signally unhealthy, rendering it objectionable as a place of destination for the colored people of the United States. We shall say nothing about other parts of the African coast, and the reasons for its location where it is : it is enough for us to know the facts as they are, to justify an unqualified objection to Liberia.

In the second place, it originated in a deep laid scheme of the slaveholders of the country, to *exterminate* the free colored of the American continent; the origin being sufficient to justify us in impugning the motives.

Thirdly and lastly—Liberia is not an Independent Republic : in fact, *it is not* an independent nation at all ; but a poor *miserable mockery—a burlesque* on a government—a pitiful dependency on the American Colonizationists, the Colonization Board at Washington city, in the District of Columbia, being the Executive and Government, and the principal man, called President, in Liberia, being the echo—a mere parrot of Rev. Robert R. Gurley, Elliot Cresson, Esq., Governor Pinney, and other leaders of the Coloniza- tion scheme—to do as they bid, and say what they tell him. This we see in all of his doings.

Does he go to France and England, and enter into solemn treaties of an honorable recognition of the independence of his country ; before his own nation has any knowledge of the result, this man called President, dispatches an official report to the Coloni- zationists of the United States, asking their gracious approval ? Does king Grando, or a party of fisher- men besiege a village and murder some of the inha- bitants, this same " President," dispatches an official report to the American Colonization Board, asking for instructions—who call an Executive Session of the Board, and immediately decide that war must be waged against the enemy, placing ten thousand dollars at his disposal—and war *actually declared in Liberia*, by virtue of the *instructions* of the *American Colonization Society*. A mockery of a government— a disgrace to the office pretended to be held—a par- ody on the position assumed. Liberia in Africa, is a mere dependency of Southern slaveholders, and American Colonizationists, and unworthy of any re- spectful consideration from us.

What would be thought of the people of Hayti, and their heads of government, if their instructions eman- ated from the American Anti-Slavery Society, or the British Foreign Missionary Board ? Should they be respected at all as a nation ? Would they be worthy of it ? Certainly not. We do not expect Liberia to be all that Hayti is; but we ask and expect of her, to have a decent respect for herself—to endeavor to be freemen instead of voluntary slaves. Liberia is no place for the colored freemen of the United States; and we dismiss the subject with a single remark of caution against any advice contained in a pamphlet, which we have not seen, written by Hon. James G. Birney, in favor of Liberian emigration. Mr. Birney is like the generality of white Americans, who suppose that we are too ignorant to understand what we want; whenever they wish to get rid of us, would drive us any where, so that we left them. Don't adhere to a word therein contained; we will think for ourselves. Let Mr. Birney go his way, and we will go ours. This is one of those confounded gratuities that is forced in our faces at every turn we make. We dismiss it without further comment— and with it Colonization *in toto*—and Mr. Birney *de facto*.

But to return to emigration: Where shall we go? We must not leave this continent; America is our destination and our home.

That the continent of America seems to have been designed by Providence as an asylum for all the various nations of the earth, is very apparent. From the earliest discovery, various nations sent a representation here, either as adventurers and speculators, or employed seamen and soldiers, hired to do the work of their employers. And among the earliest and most numerous class who found their way to the New World, were those of the African race. And

it is now ascertained to our mind, beyond a peradventure, that when the continent was discovered,
there were found in Central America, a tribe of the
black race, of fine looking people, having characteristics of color and hair, identifying them originally
of the African race—no doubt being a remnant of
the Africans who, with the Carthaginian expedition,
were adventitiously cast upon this continent, in their
memorable excursion to the " Great Island," after
sailing many miles distant to the West of the Pillars
of Hercules.

We are not inclined to be superstitious, but say,
that we can see the " finger of God" in all this ; and
if the European race may with propriety, boast and
claim, that this continent is better adapted to their
development, than their own father-land ; surely, it
does not necessarily detract from our father-land, to
claim the superior advantages to the African race, to
be derived from this continent. But be that as it
may, the world belongs to mankind—his common
Father created it for his common good—his temporal
destiny is here ; and our present warfare, is not upon
European rights, nor for European countries ; but for
the common rights of man, based upon the great principles of common humanity—taking our chance in
the world of rights, and claiming to have originally
more right to this continent, than the European race.
And had we no other claims than those set forth in
a former part of this work, they are sufficient to
cause every colored man on the continent, to stand
upon the soil unshaken and unmoved. The abori-

ginee of the continent, is more closely allied to us by consanguinity, than to the European—being descended from the Asiatic, whose alliance in matrimony with the African is very common—therefore, we have even greater claims to this continent on that account, and should unite and make common cause in elevation, with our similarly oppressed brother, the Indian.

The advantages of this continent are superior, because it presents every variety of climate, soil, and production of the earth, with every variety of mineral production, with all kinds of water privileges, and ocean coast on all sides, presenting every commercial advantage.   Upon the American continent we are determined to stay, in spite of every odds against us. What part of the great continent shall our destination be—shall we emigrate to the North or South?

CHAPTER XX.

THE CANADAS.

THIS is one of the most beautiful portions of North America.   Canada East, formerly known as Lower Canada, is not quite so favorable, the climate being cold and severe in winter, the springs being late, the summers rather short, and the soil not so productive.

But Canada West, formerly called Upper Canada, is equal to any portion of the Northern States. The climate being milder than that of the Northern portions of New York, Ohio, Michigan, Indiana, Illinois, or any of the States bordering on the lakes, the soil is prolific in productions of every description. Grains, vegetables, fruits, and cattle, are of the very best kind; from a short tour by the writer, in that country in the fall, 1851, one year ago, he prefers Canada West to any part of North America, as a destination for the colored people. But there is a serious objection to the Canadas — a political objection. The Canadians are descended from the same common parentage as the Americans on this side of the Lakes—and there is a manifest tendency on the part of the Canadians generally, to Americanism. That the Americans are determined to, and will have the Canadas, to a close observer, there is not a shadow of doubt; and our brethren should know this in time. This there would be no fear of, were not the Canadian people in favor of the project, neither would the Americans attempt an attack upon the provinces, without the move being favored by the people of those places.

Every act of the Americans, ostensibly as courtesy and friendship, tend to that end. This is seen in the policy pursued during the last two or three years, in the continual invitations, frequently reciprocated, that pass from the Americans to their " Canadian brethren"—always couched in affectionate language—to join them in their various celebrations, in different parts of the States. They have got them as far as Boston, and we may expect to hear of them going to New York, Philadelphia, Baltimore—and instead of the merrymaking over the beginning or ending of internal improvements, we may expect to see them ere long, wending their way to the seat of the federal government—it may be with William McKenzie, the memorable *patriot* and present member of the Colonial parliament, bearing in his hand the stars and stripes as their ensign—there to blend their voices in the loud shout of jubilee, in honor of the "bloodless victory," of Canadian annexation. This we forewarn the colored people, in time, is the inevitable and not far distant destiny of the Canadas. And let them come into the American Republic when they may, the fate of the colored man, however free before, is doomed, doomed, forever doomed. Disfranchisement, degradation, and a delivery up to slave catchers and kidnappers, are their only fate, let Canadian annexation take place when it will. The odious infamous fugitive slave law, will then be in full force with all of its terrors; and we have no doubt that fully in anticipation of this event, was the despicable law created.

Let not colored people be deceived and gulled by any visionary argument about original rights, or those of the people remaining the same as they were previous to cecession of the territory. The people can claim no rights than such as are known to exist previous to their annexation. This is manifestly the case with a large class of the former inhabitants of Mexico, who though citizens before, in the full exercise of their rights as such, so soon as the cecession of the territory took place, lost them entirely, as they could claim only such as were enjoyed by the people of a similar class, in the country to which they made their union. The laudatories heaped upon the Americans, within the hearing of the writer, while traveling the provinces the last fall, by one of the Canadian officiaries, in comparing their superior intelligence to what he termed the "stupid aristocracy," then returning from the Boston celebration, where there was a fair opportunity of comparing the intellect of their chief magis· trate, his excellency, Lord Elgin, governor-general of the Canadas, and Sir Allen Napier McNab, knigh* baronet with that of some of the "plain republicans" who were present on the occasion, were extravagant. The Canadians generally were perfectly carried away with delight at their reception. They reminded us of some of our poor brethren, who had just made their escape from Southern bondage, and for the first time in their life, had been taken by the hand by a white man, who acknowledged them as equals. They don't know when to stop talking about it, they really annoy one with extravagant praises of them. This was the way with those gentlemen; and we dare predict, that from what we heard on that occasion, that Mr. McKenzie nor Big Bill Johnson, hero of the Forty Islands, are no greater *patriots* than these Canadian visitors to the Boston husa! We are satisfied that the Canadas are no place of safety for the colored people of the United States; otherwise we should have no objection to them.

But to the fugitive—our enslaved brethren flying from Southern despotism—we say, until we have a more preferable place—go on to Canada. Freedom, always; liberty any place and ever—before slavery. Continue to fly to the Canadas, and swell the number of the twenty-five thousand already there. Surely the British cannot, they will not look with indifference upon such a powerful auxiliary as these brave, bold, daring men—the very flower of the South, who have hazarded every consequence, many of whom have come from Arkansas and Florida in search of freedom. Worthy surely to be free, when gained at such a venture. Go on to the North, till the South is ready to receive you—for surely, he who can make his way from Arkansas to Canada, can find his way from Kentucky to Mexico. The moment his foot touches this land South, he is free. Let the bondman but be assured that he can find the same freedom South that there is in the North; the same liberty in Mexico, as in Canada, and he will prefer going South to going North. His risk is no greater in getting there. Go either way, and he in the majority of instances must run the gauntlet of the slave states.

CHAPTER XXI.

CENTRAL AND SOUTH AMERICA AND THE WEST INDIES.

CENTRAL and South America, are evidently the ultimate destination and future home of the colored race on this continent; the advantages of which in preference to all others, will be apparent when once pointed out.*

Geographically, from the Northern extremity of Yucatan, down through Central and South America, to Cape Horn, there is a variation of climate from the twenty-second degree of North latitude, passing through the equatorial region; nowhere as warm as it is in the same latitude in Africa; to the *fifty-fifth*

---

* The native language of these countries, as well as the greater part of South America, is *Spanish*, which is the easiest of all foreign languages to learn.   It is very remarkable and worthy of note, that with a view of going to Mexico or South America, the writer several years ago paid some attention to the Spanish language ; and now, a most singular coincidence, without preunderstanding, in almost every town, where there is any intelligence among them, there are some *colored persons* of both sexes, who are studying the Spanish language. Even the Methodist and other clergymen, among them.   And we earnestly entreat all colored persons who can, to study, and have their children taught Spanish.   No foreign language will be of such *import* to colored people, in a very short time, as the Spanish. Mexico, Central and South America, importune us to speak their language ; and if nothing else, the silent indications of Cuba, urge us to learn the Spanish tongue.

degree of South latitude, including a climate as cold as that of the Hudson Bay country in British America, colder than that of Maine, or any part known to the United States of North America; so that there is every variety of climate in South, as well as North America.

In the productions of grains, fruits, and vegetables, Central and South America are also prolific; and the best of herds are here raised. Indeed, the finest Merino sheep, as well as the principal trade in rice, sugar, cotton, and wheat, which is now preferred in California to any produced in the United States—the Chilian flour—might be carried on by the people of this most favored portion of God's legacy to man. The mineral productions excel all other parts of this continent; the rivers present the greatest internal advantages, and the commercial prospects, are without a parallel on the coast of the new world.

The advantages to the colored people of the United States, to be derived from emigration to Central, South America, and the West Indies, are incomparably greater than that of any other parts of the world at present.

In the first place, there never have existed in the policy of any of the nations of Central or South America, an inequality on account of race or color, and any prohibition of rights, has generally been to the white, and not to the colored races.* To the whites,

---

* The Brazilians have formed a Colonization Society, for the purpose of colonizing free blacks to Africa. The Brazilians are Portuguese, the only nation that can be termed white, and the only one

not because they were white, not on account of their color, but because of the policy pursued by them towards the people of other races than themselves. The population of Central and South America, consist of fifteen millions two hundred and forty thousand, adding the ten millions of Mexico; twenty-five millions two hundred and forty thousand, of which vast population, but *one-seventh* are whites, or the pure European race. Allowing a deduction of one-seventh of this population for the European race that may chance to be in those countries, and we have in South and

that is a real slave holding nation in South America. Even the black and colored men have equal privileges with whites; and the action of this society will probably extend only to the sending back of such captives as may be taken from piratical slavers.

Colonization in Brazil, has doubtless been got up under the influence of United States slave holders and their abettors, such as the consuls and envoys, who are sent out to South America, by the government. Chevalier Niteroi, *charge de affaires* from Brazil near the government of Liberia, received by the President on the 28th of last January, is also charged with the mission of establishing a colony of free blacks in Liberia. The Chevalier was once a Captain in the Brazilian navy on the coast of Africa; and no doubt is conversant with the sentiments of Roberts, who was charged with the slave trade at one time. The scheme of United States slaveholders and President J. J. Roberts, their agent of Liberia, will not succeed, in establishing prejudice against the *black* race; not even in slaveholding Brazil.

We have no confidence in President Roberts of Liberia, believing him to be wholly without principle—seeking only self-aggrandizement; even should it be done, over the ruined prospects of his staggering infant country. The people of Liberia, should beware of this man. His *privy councillors* are to be found among *slaveholders* in the United States.

Central America alone, the vast colored population of *thirteen millions one hundred and seventy-seven thousand;* and including Mexico, a *colored* population on this glorious continent of *twenty-one millions, six hundred and forty thousand.*

This vast number of people, our brethren—because they are precisely the same people as ourselves and share the same fate with us, as the case of numbers of them have proven, who have been adventitiously thrown among us—stand ready and willing to take us by the hand—nay, are anxiously waiting, and earnestly importuning us to come, that they may make common cause with us, and we all share the same fate. There is nothing under heaven in our way—the people stand with open arms ready to receive us. The climate, soil, and productions—the vast rivers and beautiful sea-coast—the scenery of the landscape, and beauty of the starry heavens above—the song of the birds— the voice of the people say come—and God our Father bids us go.—Will we go? Go we must, and go we will, as there is no alternative. To remain here in North America, and be crushed to the earth in vassalage and degradation, we never will.

Talk not about religious biases—we have but one reply to make. We had rather be a Heathen *freeman,* than a Christian *slave.*

There need be no fear of annexation in these countries—the prejudices of the people are all against it, and with our influences infused among them, the aversion would be ten-fold greater. Neither need there be any fears of an attempt on the part of the United

States, at a subjugation of these countries. Policy is against it, because the United States has too many colored slaves in their midst, to desire to bring under their government, twenty-one millions of disfranchised people, whom it would cost them more to keep under subjection, than ten-fold the worth of the countries they gained. Besides, let us go to whatever parts of Central and South America we may, we shall make common cause with the people, and shall hope, by one judicious and signal effort, to assemble one day—and a glorious day it will be—in a great representative convention, and form a glorious union of South American States, "inseparably connected one and forever."

This can be done, easily done, if the proper course be pursued, and necessity will hold them together as it holds together the United States of North America —self-preservation. As the British nation serves to keep in check the Americans; so would the United States serve to keep in Union the South American States.

We should also enter into solemn treaties with Great Britain, and like other free and independent nations, take our chance, and risk consequences. Talk not of consequences ; we are now in chains; shall we shake them off and go to a land of liberty ? shall our wives and children be protected, secure, and affectionately cherished, or shall they be debased and degraded as our mothers and fathers were ? By the light of heaven, no ! By the instincts of nature, no !

Talk not about consequences. White men seek

responsibilities; shall we shun them? They brave dangers and risk consequences; shall we shrink from them? What are consequences, compared in the scale of value, with liberty and freedom; the rights and privileges of our wives and children? In defence of our liberty—the rights of my wife and children; had we the power, we would command the vault of a volcano, charged with the wrath of heaven, and blast out of existence, every thing that dared obstruct our way.

The time has now fully arrived, when the colored race is called upon by all the ties of common humanity, and all the claims of consummate justice, to go forward and take their position, and do battle in the struggle now being made for the redemption of the world. Our cause is a just one; the greatest at present that elicits the attention of the world. For it there is a remedy; that remedy is now at hand. God himself as assuredly as he rules the destinies of nations, and entereth measures into the "hearts of men," has presented these measures to us. Our race is to be redeemed; it is a great and glorious work, and we are the instrumentalities by which it is to be done. But we must go from among our oppressors; it never can be done by staying among them. God has, as certain as he has ever designed any thing, has designed this great portion of the New World, for us, the colored races; and as certain as we stubborn our hearts, and stiffen our necks against it, his protecting arm and fostering care will be withdrawn from us.

Shall we be told that we can live nowhere, but under the will of our North American oppressors; that this (the United States,) is the country most favorable to our improvement and progress? Are we incapable of self-government, and making such improvements for ourselves as we delight to enjoy after American white men have made them for themselves? No, it is not true. Neither is it true that the United States is the best country for our improvement. That country is the best, in which our manhood can be best d˄-veloped; and that is Central and South America, and the West Indies—all belonging to this glorious Continent.

Whatever may be our pretended objections to any place, whenever and wherever our oppressors go, there will our people be found in proportionate numbers. Even now could they get possession of the equatorial region of South America, there would colored men be found living on their boats and in their houses to do their menial services; but talk to them about going there and becoming men, and a thousand excuses and objections are at once raised against the climate or whatever else.

The writer, within the past few years, and as early as seventeen years ago, then being quite young, and flushed with geographical and historical speculations, introduced in a Literary Institution of Young Men, the subject of Mexican, Californian, and South American Emigration. He was always hooted at, and various objections raised: one on account of distance, and another that of climate.

He has since seen some of the same persons engage themselves to their white American oppressors—offi-

cers in the war against Mexico, exposing themselves
to the chances of the heat of day and the damp of
night—risking the dangers of the battle-field, in the
capacity of servants. And had the Americans taken
Mexico, no people would have flocked there faster than
the colored people from the United States. The same
is observed of California.

In conversation, in the city of New York, a few
weeks ago, with a colored lady of intelligence, one of
the " first families," the conversation being the elevation of the colored people, we introduced emigration
as a remedy, and Central America as the place. We
were somewhat surprised, and certainly unprepared to
receive the rebuking reply—" Do you suppose that I
would go in the woods to live for the sake of freedom?
no, indeed! if you wish to do so, go and do it. I am
free enough here !" Remarking at the same time, that
her husband was in San Francisco, and she was going
to him, as she learned that that city was quite a large
and handsome place.

We reminded her, that the industry of white men
and women, in four years' time, had made San Francisco what it is. That in 1846, before the American
emigration, the city contained about seven hundred
people, surrounded by a dense wilderness; and that
we regretted to contrast her conduct or disposition
with that of the lady of Col. Fremont, a daughter of
Senator Benton, who tenderly and indulgently raised,
in the spring after his arduous adventure across the
mountains, and almost miraculous escape, while the
country was yet a wilderness, left her comfortable

home in Missouri, and braved the dangers of the ocean, to join her husband and settle in the wilderness. That she was going now to San Francisco, because it was a populous and "fine city"—that Mrs. Fremont went, when it was a wilderness, to help to *make* a populous and fine city.

About two hours previous to the writing of the following fact, two respectable colored ladies in conversation, pleasantly disputing about the superiority of the two places, Philadelphia and New York, when one spoke of the uniform cleanliness of the streets of Philadelphia, and the dirtiness of those of New York; when the other triumphantly replied.—" The reason that our streets are so dirty is, that we do more business in one day, than you do in a month." The other acknowledged the fact with some degree of reluctance, and explained, with many "buts" as an excuse in extenuation. Here was a seeming appreciation of business and enterprise; but the query flashed through our mind in an instant, as to whether they thought for a moment, of the fact, that *they* had no interest in either city, nor its *business*. It brought forcibly to our mind, the scene of two of our oppressed brethren South, fighting each other, to prove his *master* the greatest gentleman of the two.

Let no objections be made to emigration on the ground of the difficulty of the fugitive slave, in reaching us; it is only necessary for him to know, that he has safety South, and he will find means of reaching the South, as easily as he now does the North. Have no fears about that — his redemption draws nigh, the nearer we draw to him. Central and South America, *must be our future homes.* Our oppressors will not want us to go there. They will move heaven and earth to prevent us—they will talk about us getting our rights, and offer us a territory here, and all that. It is of no use. They have pressed us to the last retreat—the die is cast —the Rubicon must be crossed—go we will, in defiance of all the slave-power in the Union. And we shall not go there, to be idle—passive spectators to an invasion of South American rights. No—go when we will, and where we may, we shall hold ourselves amenable to defend and protect the country that embraces us. We are fully able to defend ourselves, once concentrated, against any odds—and by the help of God, we will do it. We do not go, without counting the cost, cost what it may ; all that it may cost, it is worth to be free.

In going, let us have but one object—to become elevated men and women, worthy of freedom—the worthy citizens of an adopted country. What to us will be adopted—to our children will be legitimate. Go not with an anxiety of political aspirations ; but go with the fixed intention—as Europeans come to the United States—of cultivating the soil, entering into the mechanical operations, keeping of shops, carrying on merchandise, trading on land and water, improving property—in a word, to become the producers of the country, instead of the consumers.

Let young men who go, have a high object in view ; and not go with a view of becoming servants to wealthy gentlemen there ; for be assured, that they place themselves beneath all respectful consideration.

CHAPTER XXII.

NICARAGUA AND NEW GRENADA.

As it is not reasonable to suppose, that all who read this volume—especially those whom it is intended most to benefit—understand geography ; it is deemed advisable, to name some particular places, as locality of destination.

We consequently, to begin with, select NICARA-GUA, in Central America, North, and NEW GRENADA, the Northern part of South America, South of Nicaragua, as the most favorable points at present, in every particular, for us to emigrate to.

In the first place, they are the nearest points to be reached, and countries at which the California adventurers are now touching, on their route to that distant land, and not half the distance of California.

In the second place, the advantages for all kinds of enterprise, are equal if not superior, to almost any other points—the climate being healthy and highly favorable.

In the third place, and by no means the least point of importance, the British nation is bound by solemn treaty, to protect both of those nations from foreign imposition, until they are able to stand alone.

Then there is nothing in the way, but every thing in favor, and opportunities for us to rise to the full stature of manhood. Remember this fact, that in these countries, colored men now fill the highest places in the country: and colored people have the same chances there, that white people have in the United States. All that is necessary to do, is to go, and the moment your foot touches the soil, you have all the opportunities for elevating yourselves as the highest, according to your industry and merits.

Nicaragua and New Grenada, are both Republics, having a President, Senate, and Representatives of the people. The municipal affairs are well conducted; and remember, however much the customs of the country may differ, and appear strange to those you have left behind—remember that you are free; and that many who, at first sight, might think that they could not become reconciled to the new order of things, should recollect, that they were once in a situation in the United States, (in *slavery*,) where they were compelled to be content with customs infinitely more averse to their feelings and desires. And that customs become modified, just in proportion as people of different customs from different parts, settle in the same communities together.   All we ask is Liberty—the rest follows as a matter of course.

CHAPTER XXIII.

THINGS AS THEY ARE.

" And if thou boast TRUTH to utter,
SPEAK, and leave the rest to God."

IN presenting this work, we have but a single object in view, and that is, to inform the minds of the colored people at large, upon many things pertaining to their elevation, that but few among us are acquainted with. Unfortunately for us, as a body, we have been taught to believe, that we must have some person to think for us, instead of thinking for ourselves. So accustomed are we to submission and this kind of training, that it is with difficulty, even among the most intelligent of the colored people, an audience may be elicited for any purpose whatever, if the expounder is to be a colored person; and the introduction of any subject is treated with indifference, if not contempt, when the originator is a colored person. Indeed, the most ordinary white person, is almost revered, while the most qualified colored person is totally neglected. Nothing from them is appreciated.

We have been standing comparatively still for years, following in the footsteps of our friends, believing that what they promise us can be accomplished, just because they say so, although our own knowledge should long since, have satisfied us to the contrary. Because even were it possible, with the present hate and jealousy that the whites have towards us in this country, for us to gain equality of rights with them ; we never could have an equality of the exercise and enjoyment of those rights—because, the great odds of numbers are against us. We might indeed, as some at present, have the right of the elective franchise—nay, it is not the elective franchise, because the *elective franchise* makes the enfranchised, *eligible* to any position attainable ; but we may exercise the right of *voting* only, which to us, is but poor satisfaction ; and we by no means care to cherish the privilege of voting somebody into office, to help to make laws to degrade us.

In religion—because they are both *translators* and *commentators*, we must believe nothing, however absurd, but what our oppressors tell us. In Politics, nothing but such as they promulge ; in Anti-Slavery, nothing but what our white brethren and friends say we must ; in the mode and manner of our elevation, we must do nothing, but that which may be laid down to be done by our white brethren from some quarter or other ; and now, even on the subject of emigration, there are some colored people to be found, so lost to their own interest and self-respect, as to be gulled by slave owners and colonizationists, who are led to believe there is no other place in which they can become elevated, but Liberia, a government of American slave-holders, as we have shown—simply, because white men have told them so.

Upon the possibility, means, mode and manner, of our Elevation in the United States—Our Original Rights and Claims as Citizens—Our Determination not to be Driven from our Native Country—the Difficulties in the Way of our Elevation—Our Position in Relation to our Anti-Slavery Brethren—the Wicked Design and Injurious Tendency of the American Colonization Society—Objections to Liberia—Objections to Canada —Preferences to South America, &c., &c., all of which we have treated without reserve ; expressing our mind freely, and with candor, as we are determined that as far as we can at present do so, the minds of our readers shall be enlightened.   The custom of concealing information upon vital and important subjects, in which the interest of the people is involved, we do not agree with, nor favor in the least ; we have therefore, laid this cursory treatise before our readers, with the hope that it may prove instrumental in directing the attention of our people in the right way, that leads to their Elevation.   Go or stay—of course each is free to do as he pleases—one thing is certain ; our Elevation is the work of our own hands.   And Mexico, Central America, the West Indies, and South America, all present now, opportunities for the individual enterprise of our young men, who prefer to remain in the United States, in preference to going where they can enjoy real freedom, and equality of rights.   Freedom of Religion, as well as of politics, being tolerated in all of these places.

Let our young men and women, prepare themselves for usefulness and business ; that the men may enter

into merchandise, trading, and other things of importance ; the young women may become teachers of various kinds, and otherwise fill places of usefulness.
Parents must turn their attention more to the education of their children.   We mean, to educate them for
useful practical business purposes.   Educate them for
the Store and the Counting House—to do every-day
practical business.   Consult the children's propensi-
ties, and direct their education according to their in-
clinations.   It may be, that there is too great a desire
on the part of parents, to give their children a professional education, before the body of the people, are
ready for it.   A people must be a business people,
and have more to depend upon than mere help in
people's houses and Hotels, before they are either able
to support, or capable of properly appreciating the
services of professional men among them.   This has
been one of our great mistakes—we have gone in advance of ourselves.   We have commenced at the su-
perstructure of the building, instead of the foundation
—at the top instead of the bottom.   We should first
be mechanics and common tradesmen, and professions
as a matter of course would grow out of the wealth
made thereby.   Young men and women, must now
prepare for usefulness—the day of our Elevation is at
hand—all the world now gazes at us—and Central and
South America, and the West Indies, bid us come and
be men and women, protected, secure, beloved and Free.
   The branches of Education most desirable for the
preparation of youth, for practical useful every-day
life, are Arithmetic and good Penmanship, in order to

be Accountants; and a good rudimental knowledge
of Geography—which has ever been neglected, and
under estimated—and of Political Economy; which
without the knowledge of the first, no people can
ever become adventurous—nor of the second, never
will be an enterprising people. Geography, teaches a
knowledge of the world, and Political Economy, a
knowledge of the wealth of nations; or how to make
money. These are not abstruse sciences, or learning
not easily acquired or understood; but simply, common School Primer learning, that every body may
get. And, although it is the very Key to prosperity
and success in common life, but few know any thing
about it. Unfortunately for our people, so soon as
their children learn to read a Chapter in the New
Testament, and scribble a miserable hand, they are
pronounced to have "Learning enough;" and taken
away from School, no use to themselves, nor community. This is apparent in our Public Meetings, and
Official Church Meetings; of the great number of
men present, there are but few capable of filling a
Secretaryship. Some of the large cities may be an
exception to this. Of the multitudes of Merchants,
and Business men throughout this country, Europe,
and the world, few are qualified, beyond the branches
here laid down by us as necessary for business. What
did John Jacob Astor, Stephen Girard, or do the mil-
lionaires and the greater part of the merchant princes,
and mariners, know about Latin and Greek, and the
Classics? Precious few of them know any thing. In
proof of this, in 1841, during the Administration of

President Tyler, when the mutiny was detected on
board of the American Man of War Brig Somers, the
names of the Mutineers, were recorded by young
S—a Midshipman in Greek. Captain Alexander Sli-
dell McKenzie, Commanding, was unable to read them ;
and in his despatches to the Government, in justification of his policy in executing the criminals, said that
he " discovered some curious characters which he was
unable to read," &c. ; showing thereby, that that high
functionary, did not understand even the Greek Al-
phabet, which was only necessary, to have been able
to read proper names written in Greek.

What we most need then, is a good business practical Education ; because, the Classical and Professional
education of so many of our young men, before their
parents are able to support them, and community
ready to patronize them, only serves to lull their energy, and cripple the otherwise, praiseworthy efforts
they would make in life. A Classical education, is
only suited to the wealthy, or those who have a prospect of gaining a livelihood by it. The writer does
not wish to be understood, as underrating a Classical
and Professional education ; this is not his intention ;
he fully appreciates them, having had some such advantages himself ; but he desires to give a proper
guide, and put a check to the extravagant idea that is
fast obtaining, among our people especially, that a
Classical, or as it is termed, a " finished education,"
is necessary to prepare one for usefulness in life.
Let us have an education, that shall practically de-
velope our thinking faculties and manhood ; and then,

and not until then, shall we be able to vie with our oppressors, go where we may. We as heretofore, have been on the extreme ; either no qualification at all, or a Collegiate education. We jumped too far ; taking a leap from the deepest abyss to the highest summit ; rising from the ridiculous to the sublime ; without medium or intermission.

Let our young women have an education ; let their minds be well informed ; well stored with useful information and practical proficiency, rather than the light superficial acquirements, popularly and fashionably called accomplishments. We desire accomplishments, but they must be *useful.*

Our females must be qualified, because they are to be the mothers of our children. As mothers are the first nurses and instructors of children ; from them children consequently, get their first impressions, which being always the most lasting, should be the most correct. Raise the mothers above the level of degradation, and the offspring is elevated with them. In a word, instead of our young men, transcribing in their blank books, recipes for *Cooking ;* we desire to see them making the transfer of *Invoices of Merchandise.* Come to our aid then ; the *morning* of our *Redemption* from degradation, adorns the horizon.

In our selection of individuals, it will be observed, that we have confined ourself entirely to those who occupy or have occupied positions among the whites, consequently having a more general bearing as useful contributors to society at large. While we do not pretend to give all such worthy cases, we gave such as we possessed information of, and desire it to be understood, that a large number of our most intelligent and worthy men and women, have not been named, because from their more private position in community, it was foreign to the object and design of this work. If we have said aught to offend, "take the will for the deed," and be assured, that it was given with the purest of motives, and best intention, from a true hearted man and brother; deeply lamenting the sad fate of his race in this country, and sincerely desiring the elevation of man, and submitted to the serious consideration of all, who favor the promotion of the cause of God and humanity.

CHAPTER XXIV.

A GLANCE AT OURSELVES—CONCLUSION.

With broken hopes—sad devastation;
A race *resigned* to DEGRADATION !

WE have said much to our young men and women, about their vocation and calling; we have dwelt much upon the menial position of our people in this country. Upon this point we cannot say too much, because there is a seeming satisfaction and seeking after such positions manifested on their part, unknown to any other people. There appears to be, a want of a sense of propriety or *self-respect*, altogether inexplicable;

because young men and women among us, many of whom have good trades and homes, adequate to their support, voluntarily leave them, and seek positions, such as servants, waiting maids, coachmen, nurses, cooks in gentlemens' kitchen, or such like occupations, when they can gain a livelihood at something more respectable, or elevating in character. And the worse part of the whole matter is, that they have become so accustomed to it, it has become so "fashionable," that it seems to have become second nature, and they really become offended, when it is spoken against.

Among the German, Irish, and other European peasantry who come to this country, it matters not what they were employed at before and after they come ; just so soon as they can better their condition by keeping shops, cultivating the soil, the young men and women going to night-schools, qualifying themselves for usefulness, and learning trades—they do so. Their first and last care, object and aim is, to better their condition by raising themselves above the condition that necessity places them in. We do not say too much, when we say, as an evidence of the deep degradation of our race, in the United States, that there are those among us, the wives and daughters, some of the *first ladies*, (and who dare say they are not the "first," because they belong to the "first class" and associate where any body among us can ?) whose husbands are industrious, able and willing to support them, who voluntarily leave home, and become chamber-maids, and stewardesses, upon vessels and steamboats, in all probability, to enable them to obtain some more fine or costly article of dress or furniture.

We have nothing to say against those whom *necessity* compels to do these things, those who can do no better; we have only to do with those who can, and will not, or do not do better. The whites are always in the advance, and we either standing still or retrograding; as that which does not go forward, must either stand in one place or go back. The father in all probability is a farmer, mechanic, or man of some independent business ; and the wife, sons and daughters, are chamber-maids, on vessels, nurses and waiting-maids, or coachmen and cooks in families. This is retrogradation. The wife, sons, and daughters should be elevated above this condition as a necessary consequence.

If we did not love our race superior to others, we would not concern ourself about their degradation ; for the greatest desire of our heart is, to see them stand on a level with the most elevated of mankind. No people are ever elevated above the condition of their *females* ; hence, the condition of the *mother* determines the condition of the child. To know the position of a people, it is only necessary to know the *condition* of their *females ;* and despite themselves, they cannot rise above their level. Then what is our condition? Our *best ladies* being washerwomen, chamber-maids, children's traveling nurses, and common house servants, and menials, we are all a degraded, miserable people, inferior to any other people as a whole, on the face of the globe.

These great truths, however unpleasant, must be brought before the minds of our people in its true and proper light, as we have been too delicate about them, and too long concealed them for fear of giving offence. It would have been infinitely better for our race, if these facts had been presented before us half a century ago—we would have been now proportionably benefitted by it.

As an evidence of the degradation to which we have been reduced, we dare premise, that this chapter will give offence to many, very many, and why ? Because they may say, " He dared to say that the occupation of a *servant* is a degradation." It is not necessarily degrading; it would not be, to one or a few people of a kind ; but a *whole race of servants* are a degradation to that people.

Efforts made by men of qualifications for the toiling and degraded millions among the whites, neither gives offence to that class, nor is it taken unkindly by them ; but received with manifestations of gratitude ; to know that they are thought to be, equally worthy of, and entitled to stand on a level with the elevated classes ; and they have only got to be informed of the way to raise themselves, to make the effort and do so as far as they can. But how different with us. Speak of our position in society, and it at once gives insult. Though we are servants ; among ourselves we claim to be *ladies* and *gentlemen*, equal in standing, and as the popular expression goes, " Just as good as any body" —and so believing, we make no efforts to raise above the common level of menials ; because the *best* being in that capacity, all are content with the position. We cannot at the same time, be domestic and lady; servant and gentleman. We must be the one or the other. Sad, sad indeed, is the thought, that hangs drooping in our mind, when contemplating the picture drawn before us. Young men and women, " we write these things unto you, because ye are strong," because the writer, a few years ago, gave unpardonable offence to many of the young people of Philadelphia and other places, because he dared tell them, that he thought too much of them, to be content with seeing them the servants of other people. Surely, she that could be the mistress, would not be the maid; neither would he that could be the master, be content with being the servant; then why be offended, when we point out to you, the way that leads from the menial to the mistress or the master. All this we seem to reject with fixed determination, repelling with anger, every effort on the part of our intelligent men and women to elevate us, with true Israelitish degradation, in reply to any suggestion or proposition that may be offered, " Who made thee a ruler and judge ?"

The writer is no " Public Man," in the sense in which this is understood among our people, but simply an humble individual, endeavoring to seek a livelihood by a profession obtained entirely by his own efforts, without relatives and friends able to assist him; except such friends as he gained by the merit of his course and conduct, which he here gratefully acknowledges; and whatever he has accomplished, other young men may, by making corresponding efforts, also accomplish.

We have advised an emigration to Central and South America, and even to Mexico and the West Indies, to those who prefer either of the last named places, all of which are free countries, Brazil being the only real slave-holding State in South America— there being nominal slavery in Dutch Guiana, Peru, Buenos Ayres, Paraguay, and Uraguay, in all of which places colored people have equality in social, civil, political, and religious privileges; Brazil making it punishable with death to import slaves into the empire.

Our oppressors, when urging us to go to Africa, tell us that we are better adapted to the climate than they—that the physical condition of the constitution of colored people better endures the heat of warm climates than that of the whites; this we are willing to *admit*, without argument, without adducing the physiological reason why, that colored people can and do stand warm climates better than whites; and find an answer fully to the point in the fact, that they also stand *all other* climates, cold, temperate, and modified, that white people can stand; therefore, according to our oppressors' own showing, we are a *superior race*, being endowed with properties fitting us for *all parts* of the earth, while they are only adapted to *certain* parts. Of course, this proves our right and duty to live wherever we may *choose ;* while the white race may only live where they *can.* We are content with the fact, and have ever claimed it. Upon this rock, they and we shall ever agree.

Of the West India Islands, Santa Cruz, belonging

to Denmark; Porto Rico, and Cuba with its little adjuncts, belonging to Spain, are the only slave-holding Islands among them—three-fifths of the whole population of Cuba being colored people, who cannot and will not much longer endure the burden and the yoke. They only want intelligent leaders of their own color, when they are ready at any moment to charge to the conflict—to liberty or death. The remembrance of the noble mulatto, PLACIDO, the gentleman, scholar, poet, and intended Chief Engineer of the Army of Liberty and Freedom in Cuba; and the equally noble black, CHARLES BLAIR, who was to have been Commander-in-Chief, who were shamefully put to death in 1844, by that living monster, Captain General O'Donnell, is still fresh and indelible to the mind of every bondman of Cuba.

In our own country, the United States, there are *three million five hundred thousand slaves;* and we, the nominally free colored people, are *six hundred thousand* in number; estimating one-sixth to be men, we have *one hundred thousand.* able bodied freemen, which will make a powerful auxiliary in any country to which we may become adopted—an ally not to be despised by any power on earth. We love our country, dearly love her, but she don't love us—she despises us, and bids us begone, driving us from her embraces; but we shall not go where she desires us; but when we do go, whatever love we have for her, we shall love the country none the less that receives us as her adopted children.

For the want of business habits and training, our

energies have become paralyzed; our young men never think of business, any more than if they were so many bondmen, without the right to pursue any calling they may think most advisable. With our people in this country, dress and good appearances have been made the only test of gentleman and lady-ship, and that vocation which offers the best opportunity to dress and appear well, has generally been preferred, however menial and degrading, by our young people, without even, in the majority of cases, an effort to do better; indeed, in many instances, refusing situations equally lucrative, and superior in position; but which would not allow as much display of dress and personal appearance. This, if we ever expect to rise, must be discarded from among us, and a high and respectable position assumed.

One of our great temporal curses is our consummate poverty. We are the poorest people, as a class, in the world of civilized mankind—abjectly, miserably poor, no one scarcely being able to assist the other. To this, of course, there are noble exceptions; but that which is common to, and the very process by which white men exist, and succeed in life, is unknown to colored men in general. In any and every considerable community may be found, some one of our white fellow-citizens, who is worth more than all the colored people in that community put together. We consequently have little or no efficiency. We must have means to be practically efficient in all the undertakings of life; and to obtain them, it is necessary that we should be engaged in lucrative pursuits,

trades, and general business transactions. In order
to be thus engaged, it is necessary that we should
occupy positions that afford the facilities for such
pursuits. To compete now with the mighty odds of
wealth, social and religious preferences, and political
influences of this country, at this advanced stage of
its national existence, we never may expect. A new
country, and new beginning, is the only true, rational,
politic remedy for our disadvantageous position; and
that country we have already pointed out, with triple
golden advantages, all things considered, to that of
any country to which it has been the province of
man to embark.

Every other than we, have at various periods of necessity, been a migratory people; and all when oppressed, shown a greater abhorrence of oppression,
if not a greater love of liberty, than we. We cling
to our oppressors as the objects of our love. It is
true that our enslaved brethren are here, and we have
been led to believe that it is necessary for us to remain, on that account. Is it true, that all should remain in degradation, because a part are degraded?
We believe no such thing. We believe it to be the
duty of the Free, to elevate themselves in the most
speedy and effective manner possible; as the redemption of the bondman depends entirely upon the elevation of the freeman; therefore, to elevate the free
colored people of America, anywhere upon this continent; forebodes the speedy redemption of the slaves.
We shall hope to hear no more of so fallacious a doctrine—the necessity of the free remaining in degrada-

tion, for the sake of the oppressed. Let us apply, first, the lever to ourselves; and the force that elevates us to the position of manhood's considerations and honors, will cleft the manacle of every slave in the land.

When such great worth and talents—for want of a better sphere—of men like Rev. Jonathan Robinson, Robert Douglass, Frederick A. Hinton, and a hundred others that might be named, were permitted to expire in a barber-shop; and such living men as may be found in Boston, New York, Philadelphia, Baltimore, Richmond, Washington City, Charleston, (S. C.) New Orleans, Cincinnati, Louisville, St. Louis, Pittsburg, Buffalo, Rochester, Albany, Utica, Cleveland, Detroit, Milwaukie, Chicago, Columbus, Zanesville, Wheeling, and a hundred other places, confining themselves to Barber-shops and waiterships in Hotels ; certainly the necessity of such a course as we have pointed out, must be cordially acknowledged ; appreciated by every brother and sister of oppression ; and not rejected as heretofore, as though they preferred inferiority to equality. These minds must become " unfettered," and have "space to rise." This cannot be in their present positions. A continuance in any position, becomes what is termed " Second Nature ;" it begets an *adaptation*, and *reconciliation* of *mind* to such condition. It changes the whole physiological condition of the system, and adapts man and woman to a higher or lower sphere in the pursuits of life. The offsprings of slaves and peasantry, have the general characteristics

of their parents; and nothing but a different course
of training and education, will change the character.

The slave may become a lover of his master, and
learn to forgive him for continual deeds of maltreat-
ment and abuse; just as the Spaniel would couch and
fondle at the feet that kick him; because he has been
taught to reverence them, and consequently, becomes
adapted in body and mind to his condition.   Even the
shrubbery-loving Canary, and lofty-soaring Eagle,
may be tamed to the cage, and learn to love it from
habit of confinement.   It has been so with us in our
position among our oppressors; we have been so
prone to such positions, that we have learned to love
them.   When reflecting upon this all important, and
to us, all absorbing subject; we feel in the agony and
anxiety of the moment, as though we could cry out in
the language of a Prophet of old: " Oh that my head
were waters, and mine eyes a fountain of tears, that
I might weep day and night for the" degradation
" of my people!   Oh that I had in the wilderness a
lodging place of way-faring men; that I might leave
my people, and go from them!"

The Irishman and German in the United States, are
very different persons to what they were when in Ireland and Germany, the countries of their nativity.
There their spirits were depressed and downcast; but
the instant they set their foot upon unrestricted soil;
free to act and untrammeled to move; their physical
condition undergoes a change, which in time becomes
physiological, which is transmitted to the offspring,
who when born under such circumstances, is a deci-

dedly different being to what it would have been, had it been born under different circumstances.

A child born under oppression, has all the elements of servility in its constitution; who when born under favorable circumstances, has to the contrary, all the elements of freedom and independence of feeling. Our children then, may not be expected, to maintain that position and manly bearing; born under the unfavorable circumstances with which we are surrounded in this country; that we so much desire. To use the language of the talented Mr. Whipper, " they cannot be raised in this country, without being stoop shouldered." Heaven's pathway stands unobstructed, which will lead us into a Paradise of bliss. Let us go on and possess the land, and the God of Israel will be our God.

The lessons of every school book, the pages of every history, and columns of every newspaper, are so replete with stimuli to nerve us on to manly aspirations, that those of our young people, who will now refuse to enter upon this great theatre of Polynesian adventure, and take their position on the stage of Central and South America, where a brilliant engagement, of certain and most triumphant success, in the drama of human equality awaits them; then, with the blood of *slaves*, write upon the lintel of every door in sterling Capitals, to be gazed and hissed at by every passer by—

> Doomed by the Creator
> To servility and degradation;
> The SERVANT of the *white man*,
> And despised of every nation!

APPENDIX.

A PROJECT FOR AN EXPEDITION OF ADVENTURE, TO THE EASTERN COAST OF AFRICA.

———

EVERY people should be the originators of their own designs, the projector of their own schemes, and creators of the events that lead to their destiny—the consummation of their desires.

Situated as we are, in the United States, many, and almost insurmountable obstacles present themselves. We are four-and-a-half millions in numbers, free and bond; six hundred thousand free, and three-and-a-half millions bond.

We have native hearts and virtues, just as other nations; which in their pristine purity are noble, potent, and worthy of example. We are a nation within a nation;—as the Poles in Russia, the Hungarians in Austria, the Welsh, Irish, and Scotch in the British dominions.

But we have been, by our oppressors, despoiled of our purity, and corrupted in our native characteristics, so that we have inherited their vices, and but few of their virtues, leaving us in character, really a *broken people.*

Being distinguished by complexion, we are still singled out—although having merged in the habits and customs of our oppressors—as a distinct nation of people; as the

(209)

Poles, Hungarians, Irish, and others, who still retain their native peculiarities, of language, habits, and various other traits. The claims of no people, according to established policy and usage, are respected by any nation, until they are presented in a national capacity.

To accomplish so great and desirable an end, there should be held, a great representative gathering of the colored people of the United States; not what is termed a National Convention, represented en masse, such as have been, for the last few years, held at various times and places; but a true representation of the intelligence and wisdom of the colored freemen; because it will be futile and an utter failure, to attempt such a project without the highest grade of intelligence.

No great project was ever devised without the consultation of the most mature intelligence, and discreet discernment and precaution.

To effect this, and prevent intrusion and improper representation, there should be a CONFIDENTIAL COUNCIL held; and circulars issued, only to such persons as shall be *known* to the projectors to be equal to the desired object.

The authority from whence the call should originate, to be in this wise:—The originator of the scheme, to impart the contemplated Confidential Council, to a limited number of known, worthy gentlemen, who agreeing with the project, endorse at once the scheme, when becoming joint proprietors in interest, issue a *Confidential Circular*, leaving blanks for *date, time,* and *place* of *holding* the Council; sending them to trusty, worthy, and suitable colored freemen, in all parts of the United States, and the Canadas, inviting them to attend; who when met in Council, have the right to project any scheme they may think proper for the general good of the whole people—provided, that the project is laid before them after its maturity.

By this Council to be appointed, a Board of Commissioners, to consist of three, five, or such reasonable number as may be decided upon, one of whom shall be chosen as Principal or Conductor of the Board, whose duty and business shall be, to go on an expedition to the EASTERN COAST OF AFRICA, to make researches for a suitable location on that section of the coast, for the settlement of colored adventurers from the United States, and elsewhere. Their mission should be to all such places as might meet the approbation of the people; as South America, Mexico, the West Indies, &c.

The Commissioners all to be men of decided qualifications; to embody among them, the qualifications of physician, botanist, chemist, geologist, geographer, and surveyor, —having a sufficient knowledge of these sciences, for practical purposes.

Their business shall be, to make a topographical, geographical, geological, and botanical examination, into such part or parts as they may select, with all other useful information that may be obtained; to be recorded in a journal kept for that purpose.

The Council shall appoint a permanent Board of Directors, to manage and supervise the doings of the Commissioners, and to whom they shall be amenable for their doings, who shall hold their office until successors shall be appointed.

A National Confidential Council, to be held once in three years; and sooner, if necessity or emergency should demand it; the Board of Directors giving at least three months' notice, by circulars and newspapers. And should they fail to perform their duty, twenty-five of the representa-

But a few years will witness a development of gold, precious metals, and minerals in Eastern Africa, the Moon and Kong Mountains, ten-fold greater than all the rich productions of California.

There is one great physiological fact in regard to the colored race—which, while it may not apply to all colored persons, is true of those having black skins—that they can bear *more different* climates than the white race. They bear *all* the temperates and extremes, while the other can only bear the temperates and *one* of the extremes. The black race is endowed with natural properties, that adapt and fit them for temperate, cold, and hot climates; while the white race is only endowed with properties that adapt them to temperate and cold climates; being unable to stand the warmer climates; in them, the white race cannot work, but become perfectly indolent, requiring somebody to work for them—and these, are always people of the black race.

The black race may be found, inhabiting in healthful improvement, every part of the globe where the white race reside; while there are parts of the globe where the black race reside, that the white race cannot live in health.

What part of mankind is the "denizen of every soil, and the lord of terrestrial creation," if it be not the black race? The Creator has indisputably adapted us for the "denizens of *every soil*," all that is left for us to do, is to *make* ourselves the "*lords* of terrestrial creation." The land is ours—there it lies with inexhaustible resources; let us go and possess it. In Eastern Africa must rise up a nation, to whom all the world must pay commercial tribute.

We must MAKE an ISSUE, CREATE an EVENT, and ESTABLISH a NATIONAL POSITION for OURSELVES; and never may expect to be respected as men and women, until we have undertaken, some fearless, bold, and adventurous deeds of daring—contending against every odds—regardless of every consequence.

THE END.